# The
# Weekend
# Kitchen

# The Weekend Kitchen

Menus and Recipes
for Relaxed Entertaining and
Family Fun

Illustrations by Steve Salerno

## Joanne Lamb Hayes and Bonnie Tandy Leblang

Harmony Books ◆◆ New York

To Heather, Claire, Bryan,
and Eric

Published by Harmony Books, a division of Crown Publishers, Inc., 201 East 50th Street, New York, New York, 10022. Member of the Crown Publishing Group.

HARMONY and colophon are trademarks of Crown Publishers, Inc.

Manufactured in the United States of America

Book design by Nancy Kenmore

Library of Congress Cataloging-in-Publication Data

Hayes, Joanne Lamb.
    The weekend kitchen / by Joanne Lamb Hayes and Bonnie Tandy Leblang.
    Includes index.
    1. Cookery.   I. Leblang, Bonnie Tandy.   II. Title.
TX714.H39   1992
641.5—dc20                                          91-15330
                                                    CIP

ISBN 0-517-58328-3

10  9  8  7  6  5  4  3  2  1

First Edition

# CONTENTS

Chapter

SATURDAY MIDDAY • 35

Three

Chapter

# SUNDAY
# AFTERNOON AND
# EVENING • 89

Six

# INTRODUCTION

Today, people's lives move at such a fast pace that midweek cooking gets pushed to the back burner. When the weekend comes, there is more time to make meals important. Food shopping and cooking together are times to enjoy; a weekend meal at home is an event to savor, a memory to last through the next busy week. With this in mind, we've created *The Weekend Kitchen,* a helpful guide for today's busy cooks—men or women, singles, couples, or families. It is for quiet weekends together, busy weekends with friends, family weekends with the kids in the kitchen, and weekends that make ready for the busy week ahead. The menus offer many options for weekend cooking and reflect today's health and nutrition concerns in the most delicious way.

*The Weekend Kitchen* contains seven chapters of menus; within each menu you'll find recipes, techniques, and suggestions for the foods you want to prepare from Friday night through Sunday evening. Each menu includes timesaving strategies that will make your weekend in the kitchen a joy. The seventh chapter, "Weekend Dinners That Make Weekdays Easier," contains menus for those days when you can spend some time preparing things for the coming week. And the final chapter, "The Weekend Bakeshop," is a compendium of basic recipes for all the baked goods included in the menus. Because of the wide range of products it covers and the many variations for each, this section could stand alone as the only recipe source you will need for years of weekend baking.

The hustle and bustle of weekday routines changes to a more relaxed pace as the weekend nears. Friday nights become the turning point from the harried workweek to the more pleasant weekend, which might mean relaxing in front of the TV with the kids, enjoying a light supper before a roaring fire, driving to your weekend home in the country, or casually entertaining friends.

As we continue through the weekend, we've put together menus and recipes for each meal. We've included lots of strategic tips to help you work through the recipes with ease—things that we, as food writers, often do but for some reason rarely bother to print (things such as making twice as much rice as we need, freezing half, and at a later time pouring boiling water over it to thaw it quickly for an instant meal). Our recipes are not long and unwieldy and the margins are filled with hints to make the preparation even easier. We hope you will use these ideas as a springboard for making each of our recipes your own by substituting or omitting an ingredient or garnish and creating a family tradition. And, to help you locate and use the specific information that we've included in the margins, we have marked them with the following symbols:

*For your information*—definitions, historical information, safety tips, and any other tidbits of information we felt might be useful or interesting to you

*Kid stuff*—items that would be fun to make along with kids, or that kids can do by themselves

*Preparation help*—suggestions for making the recipes ahead of time, storage ideas, and freezing information, when applicable

*Helpful hints*—shortcuts, substitutes for when you are missing an ingredient or want a slightly different result, and other possible uses for the recipe item. We've also included tips to help you with a recipe, as well as lots of presentation ideas.

Also in the margins are short, succinct recipes that are usually as quick to make as they are to read.

If you have children, cooking with them during the weekend is not only fun but educational. They'll learn about foods and how to cook them. And, without even realizing it, they'll also learn about chemistry, reading, and even math. If families cook together, the children will grow up with an understanding of and appreciation for good food. Otherwise, we may end up with future generations knowing only how to microwave frozen, already-prepared foods. Many of our recipes are easy enough to be prepared by children; supervision is necessary, but the rewards are worth it.

*The Weekend Kitchen* is for life as we know it in the 1990s. We hope you, your family, and friends will enjoy it as much as we and ours have.

# FRIDAY EVENING

*chapter* *One*

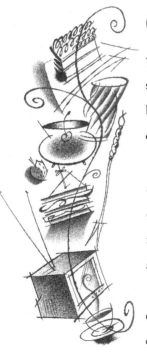

On Friday evening, you get home from work, try to toss together a meal, and sit down to enjoy it. By the time you're finished eating, you're ready to sleep until Saturday. This scenario occurs far too often, but in fact Friday can be the relaxing beginning to an enjoyable weekend, not just the exhausting end of the week.

To help you ease into the weekend, we've included a delicious assortment of menus low in work but high in flavor. Savor a cheese fondue by a roaring fire, club sandwiches with the children in front of the TV, or a light supper to enjoy at home or to carry along and enjoy after a long drive to the country.

In fact, with these plan-ahead, strategy-filled menus, Friday evenings can be so painless you could even invite some friends over to enjoy the commencement of the weekend.

# READY-WHEN-YOU-ARE SUPPER

*Parmesan Bread*

*Pasta Salad Niçoise*

*Wild Blueberry Cake*
(see page 122)

For a perfect start to a weekend, invite some friends over for a relaxing meal and lots of good conversation. To make entertaining on Friday night easier, clean up the house, chill some wine, and set the table on Thursday evening. The table needs nothing more than colorful place mats, napkins, dinner plates, and silverware. As a centerpiece, pick flowers from your garden, stop and buy some on the way home from work, or use a bowl of fresh fruit. If you've still got energy, make the pasta salad, start the Parmesan Bread, and bake the cake. If you're organized, there's not much to do on Friday evening except remove the pasta salad from the refrigerator and garnish it, then heat the bread. It couldn't be much simpler!

If you're not that organized, not to worry. Just do whatever—if anything—you can ahead, then give those who like to help a knife and cutting board and have them pitch in. Make the dinner preparation part of the party, then sit down to enjoy the beginning of the weekend.

If you have been invited to a friend's house for the weekend, pack this entire meal into the car and bring it with you as a house gift. You're sure to be invited back.

## Parmesan Bread

6 servings

| | |
|---|---|
| 1 loaf fresh French or Italian bread, sliced in half lengthwise | Unsalted butter, at room temperature<br>Freshly grated Parmesan cheese |

Preheat the oven to 375° F.

Spread both cut sides of the bread with the butter and sprinkle with Parmesan. Place both halves into the oven, cut side up, and bake until golden, 3 to 5 minutes. Serve hot.

### FOR SPRINKLING ON PARMESAN BREAD

- **C**araway, poppy, or sesame seeds
- **C**hopped black olives (preferably Greek kalamata or Italian)
- **S**hredded cheese (Jarlsberg, cheddar, jalapeño Monterey Jack)
- **1** to 2 cloves finely minced garlic

To make ahead, butter and sprinkle cheese on the bread, wrap in aluminum foil, and refrigerate for up to 1 day ahead or freeze for up to 3 months. From the refrigerator, bake 2 minutes longer; the freezer, 7 minutes longer.

For an attractive presentation, serve in a linen-lined basket or on a wooden cutting board.

If desired, spread the bread with olive oil instead of the butter.

Our recipes call for unsalted butter. If you usually have salted butter on hand, feel free to substitute it and reduce the salt in the recipe a little bit.

Easy for kids to make.

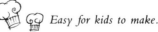

To set their color, partially cook the green beans in boiling water just until bright green and tender, about 5 minutes. Chill under cold running water to stop the cooking, drain, then wrap in a linen towel and refrigerate until needed.

To make ahead, combine the pasta and marinated ingredients the day before. Refrigerate. Garnish just before serving.

# Pasta Salad Niçoise

4 to 6 servings

Olive oil

One 6-ounce jar marinated artichoke hearts, drained and sliced, with liquid reserved

2 tablespoons red wine vinegar

2 tablespoons minced fresh parsley

1 tablespoon freshly squeezed lemon juice

2 cloves garlic, minced

$\frac{1}{2}$ teaspoon dried oregano leaves

Salt and freshly ground black pepper to taste

1 medium-size onion, sliced paper thin (about 1 cup)

$\frac{1}{3}$ cup pitted black olives, sliced into rounds

One 7-ounce can tuna, well drained and flaked

$\frac{1}{2}$ pound ($3\frac{1}{3}$ cups) spiral pasta (fusilli)

$\frac{1}{2}$ pound green beans, trimmed, partially cooked, and cut into 2-inch pieces

1 to 2 hard-cooked eggs, sliced, for garnish (optional)

2 ripe tomatoes cut into wedges, for garnish (optional)

4 to 6 anchovy fillets, for garnish (optional)

Add enough olive oil to the reserved artichoke liquid to make ¹/₂ cup. To make the dressing, add the vinegar, parsley, lemon juice, garlic, oregano, salt, and pepper to the olive oil and artichoke liquid. Blend well.

Combine the artichoke hearts, onion, olives, and tuna in a large bowl with half the marinade. Let marinate at room temperature while preparing the pasta, or for a few hours in the refrigerator.

Cook the pasta according to the package directions. Drain, rinse with cold water, drain again, then add the marinated tuna mixture. Refrigerate until an hour before serving.

Toss in the green beans and the remaining dressing just before serving (the acid in the vinegar and lemon juice alters the bright color to a drab olive green). Garnish with the eggs, tomatoes, and anchovies, if desired. Serve at room temperature.

### FREEZING PASTA

*Cook the pasta ahead and freeze it. When ready to use, place the pasta in a colander, pour hot water over it, and drain before tossing with the marinated vegetables or a favorite sauce.*

*Or place the frozen pasta in a microwave-safe serving bowl, cover with a plate, and microwave until warmed through; the time needed depends on the amount of pasta and the wattage of your oven.*

*Cheese Fondue*

*Romaine Lettuce and Italian Tomato Salad*

*Chocolate Fondue with Fruit, Cake, and Cookies*

# FAMILY FIRESIDE FEAST

On a cold winter Friday evening, gather the family before a roaring fire for a supper that can be put together in minutes. Eating fondue is fun. From entrée to dessert, everyone selects and dips favorite foods. In the excitement of plunging foods into the creamy cheese mixture, children will sometimes even eat vegetables they wouldn't touch if they were served on a plate.

Feel free to use any foods that you have on hand for dipping. A fondue is a good way to use up leftover meats or vegetables. Chunks of cooked chicken or sausage, as well as cooked shrimp or firm fish such as monkfish, are excellent selections.

If you feel comfortable sitting on pillows on the floor, the whole family can relax before the fire and have a leisurely meal. Set up a coffee table for the fondue pot or place it on the hearth.

# Cheese Fondue

*4 servings*

2 tablespoons all-purpose flour

½ teaspoon dry mustard

1¼ cups dry white wine or skim milk

½ pound medium-sharp cheddar cheese, coarsely shredded (about 2 cups)

¼ pound Jarlsberg cheese, coarsely shredded (about 1 cup)

¼ pound Muenster cheese, coarsely shredded (about 1 cup)

Bite-size pieces of cooked broccoli, asparagus, carrots, new potatoes, green beans, meat or seafood; chunks of French bread and Pumpernickel Bread (see page 158)

In a 1-quart saucepan, combine the flour and mustard. Gradually stir in the wine or skim milk until the mixture is uniformly blended. Heat the mixture over medium heat, stirring, until it comes to a boil. Cook the mixture 1 minute, stirring constantly.

Remove the thickened mixture from the stove and stir in the shredded cheeses until they are completely melted and the mixture is smooth. Pour into the top of a fondue pot and place it over the heat source.

To serve Cheese Fondue, arrange the vegetables, meat or seafood, and bread on a serving platter. Place the platter along with the fondue pot containing fondue in the center of the table. Give everyone a long-handled fondue fork to spear the vegetables, meat or seafood, and bread and dip them into the cheese mixture.

**ROMAINE LETTUCE AND ITALIAN TOMATO SALAD:** *A medium head of romaine lettuce will make a generous salad for 4 people. Wash the lettuce, drain it well, and tear it into bite-size pieces. Add 4 Italian tomatoes, quartered lengthwise, and pass an Italian-style vinaigrette dressing. You could offer a selection of dressings, but it is best to stay away from creamy dressings with the cheese in the fondue.*

## GOOD CHOICES FOR DIPPERS

*Strawberries*

*Kiwi slices*

*Grapes*

*Pineapple chunks*

*Banana chunks*

*(dipped in lemon juice
to prevent discoloration)*

*Cubes of pound cake
or angel food cake*

*(most other kinds
are too crumbly)*

*Almond Macaroons*

*(see page 125)*

*Meringue Cookies*

*(see page 128)*

# Chocolate Fondue with Fruit, Cake, and Cookies

4 servings

Eight 1-ounce squares
semisweet chocolate,
chopped

⅓ cup half-and-half

1 to 2 tablespoons
brandy, liqueur, or
additional half-and-
half

Fruit, cake, and cookies
for dipping

Combine the chocolate and half-and-half in the top of a double boiler. Heat over simmering water, stirring constantly, just until the chocolate is melted and the mixture is smooth. Stir in brandy. Pour the chocolate mixture into a fondue pot and place it over the heat source.

To serve, arrange a variety of fruit, cake pieces, and cookies for dipping on a plate. Give each person a small plate and a fondue fork and let them enjoy selecting and dipping their own dessert.

### Variation

*Chocolate Sauce:* For a quick and decadent chocolate sauce to serve over fresh fruit or ice cream, increase the half-and-half to ½ or ⅔ cup according to the thickness of the sauce desired, and proceed with the instructions above.

# KIDS' TV NIGHT

In many homes, Friday evening is family night, when every-one tries to catch up on what's happened during the week. To promote the conversation, have everyone join in to help make this easy-to-prepare dinner. Then, enjoy it either at the dinner table or in front of the television set, where there are lots of family shows. You don't have to just sit and watch the shows; you can use them as a springboard for conversation.

No need to make anything ahead. Our family-night meal includes a club sandwich, crispy potatoes, and mouth-watering orange-flavored blond brownies, all of which can be prepared by someone of any age. Bake the blondies after the kids get home from school; they'll be cool and ready to enjoy by the time you've finished dinner.

Have one of the kids set snack tables in the family room in front of the television, using a place mat and coordinated napkin on each. Whoever's setting the table gets to choose the colors. Make it a real family affair; everyone in the family can help.

Sliced Turkey
Junior Club

Baked Chips

Orange
Blondies
*(see page 124)*

*Easy for kids to make. Just provide them with the sliced fillings, breads, and a choice of spreads, and let them go wild.*

*Leftover turkey from a Sunday dinner (see page 98) can be sliced and frozen ahead in preparation for this meal.*

*For an attractive presentation, secure each corner with a frilled toothpick, then quarter the sandwich diagonally. If frilled toothpicks are unavailable, cover the ends of a plain toothpick with olives or pickles.*

# Sliced Turkey Junior Club

### 4 servings

| | |
|---|---|
| Mustard or mayonnaise mixed with horseradish, to taste | 8 slices turkey |
| 8 slices whole-grain bread, toasted | 4 to 8 lettuce leaves, rinsed and dried |
| | 2 ripe tomatoes, sliced |
| | 8 slices cooked bacon |

Spread the mustard or mayonnaise on each slice of toast, layer 2 slices of turkey, ¼ of the lettuce and tomatoes, and 2 slices bacon on 1 slice, top with the other. Repeat for the next 3 sandwiches. Cut and serve.

### Variations

- Use any bread you have on hand—challah, pumpernickel, rye, cracked wheat.
- Use ham, chicken, roast beef, salami, pastrami, corned beef, and/or Swiss, Roquefort, mozzarella, provolone, or any cheese.
- Add cranberry sauce, Mango Chutney (see page 72), sauerkraut, potato salad, pimiento, sliced hard-cooked eggs, cucumbers, or sliced onions.
- Spread the toast with butter, plain mayonnaise, chutney, preserves, horseradish, or yogurt.
- Make the sandwiches with 3 slices of bread for hearty teenage or adult appetites.

# Baked Chips

❦

4 servings

4 baking potatoes, scrubbed and cut into ¼-inch rounds

¼ cup olive oil

Freshly ground black pepper to taste

Salt to taste (optional)

Preheat the oven to 400° F.

Toss the potatoes with the olive oil and spread in a single layer on a rimmed baking sheet. Season with pepper. Bake for 20 minutes, remove from the oven, turn, and let rest for 5 minutes, then return to the oven for an additional 10 minutes. Sprinkle with salt, if desired. Serve hot.

Curried
Lentils
with
Basmati Rice

Sautéed
Spinach

Carrot and
Raisin Salad

Broiled
Pineapple

# MEATLESS
# MAKE-AHEAD

At the end of a long week, treat your family or friends to a vegetable feast that will wake up their taste buds for the weekend. A delicious and colorful array of fresh fruits and vegetables make this Friday-evening supper a nutritious, high-fiber, low-fat festival of flavor. Make the curried lentils a day ahead for convenience. A night in the refrigerator will allow the flavors to mellow and combine. If you put the lentils on to cook as you start Thursday night's dinner and add the finishing touches just before dishwashing, it won't seem like an extra preparation. The rest of the menu is quick to prepare and easy enough so that everyone lured to the kitchen by the aroma of the curried lentils slowly reheating can be given a job. Apple cider, a fruity white wine, or your local boutique beer would go well with this meal.

The Weekend Kitchen

# Curried Lentils with Basmati Rice

⌘

### 6 servings

## Curried Lentils

1³/₄ cups dried lentils (³/₄ pound), cleaned

4 cups water

2 teaspoons olive oil

1 small green bell pepper, coarsely chopped (about ¹/₂ cup)

1 medium-size onion, coarsely chopped (about 1 cup)

2 teaspoons freshly grated gingerroot

1 teaspoon mustard seeds

2 to 4 teaspoons curry powder

1 teaspoon dried basil

1 teaspoon salt

Two 15-ounce cans stewed tomatoes

## Basmati Rice

1¹/₂ cups Basmati or other aromatic rice

3 cups water

¹/₂ teaspoon salt

*To make Curried Lentils:* Combine the lentils and water in a 4-quart saucepan; bring to a boil over high heat. Reduce the heat and simmer, covered, until the lentils are almost tender and all of the water has been absorbed, about 30 minutes.

Meanwhile, heat the olive oil in a small skillet. Add the pepper, onion, gingerroot, and mustard seeds. Sauté, stirring, until the onion is golden brown. Stir in the curry powder, basil, and salt; set the pepper mixture aside.

Stir the pepper mixture and stewed tomatoes into the lentils. Return to a boil. Cover and cook over low heat until the lentils are very tender, 20 to 30 minutes longer.

(continued)

To clean lentils (or beans) before cooking, pick out and discard any foreign objects or discolored lentils, then rinse them well.

**CURRY POWDER:** *The English invented curry powder to try to simulate the delicious spice combinations they had enjoyed in India. To prepare your own curry powder, combine 1 teaspoon coriander seeds, 1 teaspoon cumin seeds, ¹/₂ teaspoon mustard seeds, ¹/₂ teaspoon fenugreek seeds, and ¹/₄ teaspoon whole cloves in a small heavy skillet with a lid. Cover the skillet and place it over low heat, shaking occasionally, until the seeds are aromatic, 8 to 10 minutes. Pour the seeds into a small bowl and set them aside to cool. Combine the cooled seeds with ¹/₄ teaspoon each ground mace, ground cardamom, ground cinnamon, and red pepper flakes and 1 teaspoon ground turmeric in the container of a spice mill or small food processor. Finely grind the spices together; store the curry powder in an airtight jar and use within several weeks for best flavor.*

 *Basmati rice is an aromatic rice originally imported from India and Pakistan; its name means "queen of fragrance." Aromatic rices have the delicate flavor of fresh corn, and when cooking, they smell of popcorn. American-grown Basmati, Jasmine, Texmati, popcorn, and Wild Pecan rices could be used in this recipe.*

*Cracked pepper adds visual interest as well as its peppery flavor to a recipe. If you would like to substitute regular ground pepper for cracked, use about ³/₄ teaspoon ground for every teaspoon cracked. Freshly ground pepper has a more pronounced flavor than already-ground, purchased pepper or cracked; adjust the amount used to your taste.*

*If cooked completely, 1 pound of spinach shrinks to less than a cup. This recipe is best if the spinach is slightly undercooked so the leaves do not lose all of their identity; then the volume will remain enough for 6 servings.*

 *Easy for kids to prepare.*

*To make Basmati Rice:* Combine the rice, water, and salt in a 2-quart saucepan. Bring the mixture to a boil. Reduce the heat, cover, and cook over low heat until the rice is tender and all of the water has been absorbed, about 20 minutes.

To serve, spoon the cooked rice onto a large serving platter. Spoon the lentil mixture on top, or serve each from separate casseroles.

## Sautéed Spinach

6 servings

¹/₄ cup sliced scallions
2 cloves garlic, sliced
2 tablespoons olive oil
1¹/₂ pounds young spinach leaves, washed and well drained

¹/₄ teaspoon salt
¹/₄ teaspoon cracked black pepper

In a large skillet, sauté the scallions and garlic in olive oil until the garlic is golden. Add the spinach; cover and cook for 3 to 4 minutes, stirring occasionally, until the leaves begin to wilt. Stir in the salt and pepper and serve immediately.

## Carrot and Raisin Salad

6 servings

1 pound carrots, peeled and coarsely grated (about 4 cups)
¹/₃ cup dark seedless raisins
¹/₄ cup mayonnaise

¹/₄ cup vanilla-flavored nonfat or low-fat yogurt
4 large leaves Boston or iceberg lettuce

In a large bowl, combine all of the ingredients except the lettuce. Line a 2-quart bowl with the lettuce leaves and spoon the carrot mixture into the center of it. Serve immediately or cover and refrigerate until ready to serve.

### Variations

- Delicious stuffed into whole wheat pita.
- Substitute coarsely grated turnip for half (2 cups) of the grated carrots.
- Add ½ cup chopped fresh pineapple or very well drained, canned crushed pineapple.

## Broiled Pineapple

6 servings

1 ripe fresh pineapple
¼ cup firmly packed
   light brown sugar

½ teaspoon ground
   cinnamon

Peel the pineapple and slice crosswise into 6 rounds. Remove the core from each slice with a 1-inch cookie cutter.

Preheat the broiler.

In a small bowl, combine the brown sugar and cinnamon. Arrange the pineapple slices on a broiler pan. Sprinkle with half the sugar mixture. Broil 4 inches from the heat source until golden brown on the edges, 3 or 4 minutes. Turn the pineapple slices; sprinkle with the remaining sugar mixture and broil until brown on the remaining side, 2 to 3 minutes. Serve immediately.

### Variations

- Top with vanilla frozen yogurt or ice cream.
- Substitute maple sugar or crumbled maple-sugar candies for the brown sugar.

*The pineapple became the symbol of hospitality when New England ship captains returning from the tropics each placed a pineapple on his gatepost to indicate that the master had returned and the home was now open for visitors.*

# CHAPTER
# SATURDAY MORNING
## Two

As the sun rises on Saturday morning, you glance at the clock and somehow know you don't have to jump out of bed and rush off to work. You might have to meet a friend for an early morning jog or take the kids to soccer practice, but you know it's the weekend and there's something comforting about that.

The first meal of the day can be a hearty and healthful breakfast that the whole family can make and enjoy together, such as a vegetable frittata with freshly squeezed orange juice or very special eggs with a simple fruit salad. If kids don't have outdoor activities, get them involved inside with the meal preparation. Cooking with children—no matter what the age—becomes special family time, quality time you spend together. There are tasks for every age: setting the table, squeezing oranges for juice, mixing muffin batter, making fruit salad. What's important is the unharried time together. Once family members leave the breakfast table, they're off and running to enjoy their weekend.

# HIGH-ENERGY FAMILY BREAKFAST

*Country Vegetable Frittata*

*Gingerbread Muffins*
*(see page 155)*

*Freshly Squeezed Orange Juice*

Here's a stick-to-the-ribs breakfast to start a busy day. Recruit some help to set the table and squeeze the oranges, and breakfast will be ready in no time. Measure the muffin dry ingredients the night before so all you have to do is stir in the liquids and bake them in the morning. The aroma of gingerbread baking will bring all your sleepyheads down to breakfast in a hurry.

## Country Vegetable Frittata

### 4 to 6 servings

1 large onion, thinly
   sliced (about 1¹/₂ cups)
1 *each* medium-size
   green, red, and yellow
   bell peppers, cored,
   seeded, and cut into
   julienne strips (about 2
   cups)
2 tablespoons olive oil

2 cloves garlic, minced
8 eggs
3 tablespoons milk
¹/₂ teaspoon dried thyme
   leaves
Salt and freshly ground
   black pepper to taste
¹/₃ cup freshly grated Parmesan cheese

Sauté the onion and bell peppers in the olive oil in a large ovenproof skillet over medium heat until slightly caramelized, about 25 minutes. Add the garlic and cook an additional minute.

Preheat the broiler.

Whisk together the eggs, milk, thyme, salt, and pepper. Pour the mixture into the pan and cook over low heat until the bottom is set, 3 to 4 minutes. The top should still be moist and creamy. Sprinkle the eggs with the Parmesan.

Place the skillet under the hot broiler and cook until golden and sizzling, about 2 minutes. Cut into wedges and serve the frittata hot from the skillet or at room temperature.

### Variations

*Broccoli:* Omit the peppers and onions. Instead, sauté scallions and garlic in butter. Add 2 cups of broccoli florets. Season with red pepper flakes.

*Mushroom:* Omit the peppers. Cook the onions until translucent, add 1 cup sliced mushrooms, a splash of dry sherry, and a pinch of tarragon.

 *Great for a picnic.*

*To make ahead, cook completely and serve at room temperature. Or cook the peppers, onions, and garlic, and refrigerate until ready to make the frittata.*

**FRESHLY SQUEEZED ORANGE JUICE:** *It takes 2 to 4 medium juice oranges to make 1 cup juice. As a general rule, freshly squeezed juice contains slightly—but not significantly—more vitamin C than does processed.*

# FOR KIDS OF ALL AGES

Even when on the run to take the kids to soccer, ice-skating, swimming, or dance or music lessons, there's time for a fun family breakfast. After cleaning up on Friday evening, put colorful place mats on the table in anticipation of breakfast. If your children are very young, consider using their latest artwork—protected by plastic wrap, of course—as the place mats. Use a basket of muffins for the centerpiece. Making the table attractive is just as important for breakfasting with the family as for entertaining friends.

The kids can make this entire meal with minimal supervision, or everyone can pitch in together.

# My Own Special Eggs

1 serving

| | |
|---|---|
| 1 thick slice whole wheat bread | Salt and freshly ground black pepper to taste |
| 1 egg | 1 teaspoon unsalted butter |

Using a 2-inch cookie cutter, cut out the center of the bread. Break the egg into a small bowl. Season with salt and pepper.

Heat the butter in a small skillet over medium–high heat. Place the bread in the skillet and pour the egg into the hole. Cook until the bottom of the egg is set and the bread is lightly browned, about 2 minutes. Turn and cook on the other side until the egg is set, about an additional 2 minutes.

## Variations

- Let your children select a cookie cutter of any shape. Or just cut a circle in the center of the bread. Use a shamrock cutter for St. Patrick's Day, a heart for Valentine's Day, a pumpkin for Halloween, a turkey for Thanksgiving morning, or whatever shape you have on hand.
- Scramble the egg before pouring it into the skillet.
- Add some freshly grated Parmesan cheese to the egg.
- Use thick–sliced challah bread.

*The cutouts can be used to make bread crumbs. Just process them in a blender, place into a container or sealable plastic bag, and freeze until needed. For **Italian-flavored bread crumbs:** Add freshly grated Parmesan cheese, basil, oregano, salt, and freshly ground black pepper to bread crumbs.*

*Easy for kids to make.*

*To prepare ahead, combine all the fruits except the strawberries or raspberries. Add them just before serving.*

*Easy for kids to make. Provide them with a sharp knife, cutting board, melon baller, large bowl, and, if they are beginners, knife safety guidance.*

### KNIFE SAFETY TIPS FOR YOUNGSTERS

*Keep your fingers away from the sharp edges of the knife.*

*Always pick up and handle a knife by the handle, not the blade.*

*Cut food on a cutting board, not while holding it in your hand.*

*Hold the handle of the knife with your writing hand; hold the large end of the food with your other hand, keeping your hand away from the blade.*

*Curl in the tips of your fingers when holding food to be cut with a knife.*

*Never put a knife in a dishpan of soapy water where you or others won't be able to see it.*

# Fruit Salad

4 to 6 servings

1 orange, peeled and sectioned

½ pound seedless grapes

1 cup blueberries, strawberries, or raspberries

½ fresh pineapple, peeled, cored, and cut into bite-size pieces

½ cantaloupe, seeds and rind removed, then cubed

2 tablespoons orange juice

½ cup plain nonfat yogurt

Fresh mint sprigs, for garnish (optional)

Combine all the fruits with the juice and yogurt in a bowl. For an attractive presentation, garnish with a sprig or two of fresh mint, if desired. Serve immediately.

## Variations

• Omit the yogurt.
• Use orange or other fruit-flavored yogurt.
• Use canned fruits when fresh are unavailable.
• Serve the fruit salad in seeded cantaloupe halves.

# CONTINENTAL BUFFET

The morning sun peeks through the lace curtains onto a typical European breakfast table. It sparkles upon bowls of granola, porridgelike Prepared Muesli, yogurt, and a variety of fresh fruits. Breakfasters don't need to rush down at the first sniff of coffee brewing; this breakfast is do-it-yourself and ready whenever you are, a perfect menu for Saturday mornings everywhere. If most of the menu components are assembled the night before, things need only be set out in the morning. The Cinnamon Coffee Cake could be made ahead and reheated. The scones are best hot off the grill, but the batter could be made, stored in the refrigerator for up to two hours, and baked as needed.

Homemade
Granola

Prepared
Muesli

Assorted
Fresh Fruit

Yogurt

Griddle Scones
*(see page 157)*

Cinnamon
Coffee Cake
*(see page 150)*

*If stored in an airtight container in a cool, dry place, this granola will be good for at least a month.*

*Don't serve this just as a breakfast cereal. It makes a great topping for ice cream, frozen or regular yogurt, pies, or cakes. Pack some in small plastic bags to use as trail mix or add to school lunch boxes.*

*Easy for kids to make.*

# Homemade Granola

### About 4 cups

| | |
|---|---|
| 2 cups old-fashioned rolled oats | 2 tablespoons honey |
| 1/2 cup sliced natural almonds | 2 tablespoons vegetable oil |
| 1/2 cup coarsely chopped walnuts | 2 tablespoons water |
| 1/2 cup sunflower kernels (shelled sunflower seeds) | 1/2 teaspoon ground cinnamon |
| 2 tablespoons sesame seeds | 1/4 cup dark seedless raisins |
| | 1/4 cup dried apricots, quartered |

Preheat the oven to 300° F.

Combine the oats, almonds, walnuts, sunflower kernels, and sesame seeds in a large bowl. Combine the honey, oil, water, and cinnamon in a small cup; pour it over the oat mixture and toss until everything is evenly moistened.

Spread the granola evenly over 2 rimmed cookie sheets and bake, stirring occasionally, until the oats are golden brown, 12 to 15 minutes. Remove the granola from the oven and stir in the dried fruit. Cool to room temperature and store in tight containers until ready to serve.

### Variation

*Low-fat Sugarless Granola:* Omit the honey, oil, and water and just sprinkle the cinnamon over the oat mixture. Bake, cool, and store as directed.

The Weekend Kitchen

# Prepared Muesli

About 4 cups

1 cup old-fashioned rolled oats

¼ cup oat bran

½ cup coarsely chopped dried apples

¼ cup chopped hazelnuts or almonds

1 cup skim milk

One 8-ounce container plain nonfat yogurt (1 scant cup)

One 8-ounce container vanilla-flavored low-fat yogurt (1 scant cup)

1 teaspoon vanilla extract

1½ cups fresh berries or seedless grapes, sliced fresh peaches, pears, or bananas (vary the fruit according to the season)

The day before serving, combine the oats, oat bran, apples, and nuts in a medium-size bowl. Stir in the milk, yogurts, and vanilla until the mixture is uniformly blended. Cover tightly and refrigerate overnight.

The next day, stir the mixture, top with fresh fruit, and serve.

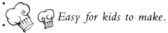 *Easy for kids to make.*

**ASSORTED FRESH FRUIT:** *Select the best seasonal fruit and serve it as simply as possible—a bowl of washed berries, washed apples, pears, peaches, nectarines, or plums on a board with a knife. Or, if you wish, you can prepare Fruit Salad (see page 26), but serve the yogurt on the side.*

**YOGURT:** *Set out an assortment of 8-ounce containers of flavored low-fat yogurts in a bowl of crushed ice.*

# HEARTY AND HEALTHY

Dried Apricot
and Chicken
Sausage

Light Strata

Tropical
Fruit Compote

Looking for something low in fat yet satisfying and delicious? This menu features some old-fashioned breakfast traditions that have been adjusted to meet today's tastes and health concerns. The tangy sweetness of dried apricot adds excitement to a low-fat chicken sausage. With no need to stuff, this sausage mixture can be formed into skinless rolls or flat patties for cooking. The strata uses egg whites and low-fat milk to make a healthier version of this custardy breakfast, brunch, or lunch dish. The Tropical Fruit Compote is so pretty that it can double as a centerpiece—but don't be surprised if people eat the arrangement.

# Dried Apricot and Chicken Sausage

8 small patties or links, 4 servings

½ cup dried apricot
    halves, finely chopped

¼ cup boiling water

1 pound ground chicken

¾ teaspoon salt

½ teaspoon dried basil

¼ to ½ teaspoon freshly
    ground black pepper

¼ teaspoon ground
    allspice

1 teaspoon vegetable oil

Combine the apricots and boiling water in a small bowl; set aside
for 5 minutes. Combine the ground chicken, salt, basil, pepper, and
allspice in a medium-size bowl. Drain off and discard any liquid
remaining with the apricots; stir the apricots into the chicken
mixture.

Shape the sausage mixture into 8 patties or links. Heat the oil in
a large skillet; add the sausages and sauté over medium heat until
well browned on one side. Turn the sausages and sauté until well
browned on the other side, 8 to 10 minutes total.

*To make ahead, wrap the shaped patties or links individually and freeze. To cook frozen sausages, place them still frozen in a hot skillet and sauté them, over low heat, 15 to 18 minutes, turning once, or until cooked through.*

*Light Jarlsberg is a low-fat version of the traditional Norwegian Jarlsberg cheese. It can be substituted for the original in most recipes.*

# Light Strata

8 slices whole-grain bread

¼ pound low-fat cheddar cheese, shredded (1 cup)

¼ pound light Jarlsberg cheese, shredded (1 cup)

¼ cup finely chopped green onion

¼ cup finely chopped red bell pepper

¼ cup finely chopped black olives

4 egg whites

2 teaspoons Dijon mustard

2½ cups skim milk

1 teaspoon Worcestershire sauce

The day before serving, lightly grease an 8-inch shallow casserole. In the casserole, combine the bread, half of the cheeses, the onion, pepper, and olives, tossing to mix uniformly. In a small bowl, beat the egg whites and mustard together until the whites are frothy. Gradually beat in the milk and Worcestershire sauce. Pour the milk mixture over the bread mixture. Top with remaining cheeses, cover, and refrigerate overnight.

The next day, preheat the oven to 350° F.

Bake the strata, uncovered, until firm in center and golden brown, 30 to 40 minutes. Serve immediately.

# Tropical Fruit Compote

*4 servings*

| | |
|---|---|
| 1 ripe fresh pineapple | 1 tablespoon passion |
| ½ large papaya (red if | fruit– or orange- |
| possible) | flavored liqueur |
| 1 navel orange | 1½ teaspoons Angostura |
| | bitters |

Wash and dry the pineapple. Slice off 2½ inches from one side, leaving the frond intact; lay down the pineapple on a serving platter, cut side up. To make a bowl from the pineapple, remove the fruit with a grapefruit knife, leaving a ½-inch rim. Cut the removed fruit into 1-inch cubes. Peel and cube the 2½-inch slice of pineapple initially removed.

Place the pineapple cubes in a medium-size bowl. Peel the papaya; discard the seeds. Cut the papaya flesh into cubes and add them to the pineapple. Working over the bowl of fruit, peel and section the orange. Add the sections to the fruit mixture. Add the liqueur and Angostura bitters and stir the mixture until it is well blended. Spoon the fruit into the prepared pineapple-shell bowl and place on a serving platter. Cover and refrigerate until ready to serve.

# *Chapter* SATURDAY MIDDAY *Three*

Saturday lunch can be an event in itself or just a quick accompaniment to your favorite activity. All week long, lunch is devoted to business—a meeting with clients, a lunchtime planning session, a quick bite at your desk, or a sandwich in the car on your way to do the family errands. Saturday lunch, though, is different—a time to share with family and friends when the only order of business is enjoying good food and one another's company. Lunch can be a southwestern tailgate feast shared with friends before a game or after a swim at the beach, a family cookout featuring the morning's farmers' market finds, a relaxed lunch at home on a lazy afternoon, or a Greek Islands picnic to be barbecued in the park. Whatever your Saturday brings, here is an abundance of ideas for midday munching—use our menus as they are suggested or mix and match ideas to fit the occasion and the foods you have on hand.

# THE SANDWICH BOARD

Choose Your
Own Sandwich

❧

Fresh Fruit

❧

Orange
Blondies
*(see page 124)*
*or*
Butter
Cookies
*(see page 126)*

❧

Iced Tea

On a hectic Saturday morning, serve sandwiches for the mid-day meal. Be sure to buy and have available an assortment of different fillings as well as many different kinds of bread. Arrange the fillings and breads on the table along with a wicker basket filled with seasonal fruit, a heaping platter of homemade cookies or brownies, and a pitcher filled with homemade iced tea. Then sit back, while everyone—including you—selects whatever they like.

# Choose Your Own Sandwich

Here are some unusual sandwich ideas to mix and match.

## Fillings

Avocado, sprouts, and sliced tomatoes with tahini dressing

Camembert with roasted peppers and Caponata (see page 95)

Curried Chicken Salad (see page 107)

Cream cheese with chopped dates and nuts

Ham, Brie, and watercress with honey-mustard dressing

Jarlsberg cheese, sliced cornichons, and Bibb lettuce with Dijon mustard

Liver pâté with sliced mushrooms and hard-cooked eggs

Meat loaf with chili sauce

Sardines with lettuce, sliced tomatoes, and red onions

Scrambled eggs with chives

Sliced turkey, Russian dressing, sauerkraut with Gruyère cheese

Smoked salmon, cream cheese, scallions, and sliced tomatoes

## Breads

Bagels

Black bread

Brioches

Corn tortillas

Cracked-wheat bread

Date-nut bread

English muffins

Five-grain bread

Flour tortillas

Pita bread

Pumpernickel Bread (see page 158)

Rye bread

Sesame or other rolls

Sourdough bread

Whole wheat bread

*You can let the sun brew your iced tea. Place 9 tea bags in a gallon jar, fill the jar with cold water, cover, and place outside in hot sunshine for 3 to 4 hours. (Be sure to refrigerate within 5 hours of starting.) Discard the tea bags and serve the tea over ice.*

**FRESH FRUIT:** *Whatever the season, fruit is always available. Just select the best.*

**ICED TEA:** *As easy as one-two-three, first pour 4 cups of boiling water over 6 tea bags, then cover and let brew for at least 3 to 5 minutes. Cool. Finally, discard the tea bags and serve the tea over ice. This makes about 1 quart.*

*Portable
Nachos and/or
Gulf Coast
Shrimp*

*Jicama Salad*

*Black Bean,
Spiced Chicken,
and Avocado
Fajitas*

*Fresh Fruit*

*Meringue
Cookies
and
Almond
Macaroons*
*(see pages 128 and 125)*

*White Sangria*

*Mexican Coffee*

# A SOUTHWESTERN TAILGATE

On a crisp autumn afternoon, meet friends in the stadium parking lot for a portable celebration of southwestern specialties. From appetizers to dessert, this tailgate buffet can be made ahead and packed for relaxed before-the-game entertaining. This lively menu doesn't have to be retired when the football season is over. It can be carried just as easily to a baseball game or tennis match, the mountains or the beach.

# Portable Nachos

6 servings

## Tomato Salsa

2 large ripe tomatoes, chopped (about 2 ½ cups)

¼ cup finely chopped scallions

One-half 4-ounce can chopped green chilies (mild or hot), drained

1 clove garlic, minced

1 tablespoon red wine vinegar

½ teaspoon sugar

¼ teaspoon salt

2 to 4 drops Tabasco

## Cheese Sauce

½ cup milk

1 tablespoon all-purpose flour

1½ cups (6 ounces) shredded jalapeño Monterey Jack cheese

1½ cups (6 ounces) shredded mild cheddar cheese

One 8-ounce bag yellow corn tortilla chips

One 8-ounce bag blue tortilla chips

*To make Tomato Salsa:* Several hours before serving, combine all the ingredients in a plastic container and refrigerate until ready to use.

*To make Cheese Sauce:* Just before ready to serve or pack for tailgate, combine the milk and flour in a 1-quart saucepan. Bring the mixture to a boil over medium heat, stirring constantly until smooth. When the mixture has thickened, stir in the cheeses and continue cooking just until the cheeses are melted and the mixture is smooth.

Serve cheese sauce and salsa with chips.

*Italian tomatoes are better than regular tomatoes for making salsa because they are meatier. To remove as many seeds as possible, cut them into quarters and shake out the seeds while gently squeezing or remove them with a spoon.*

# Gulf Coast Shrimp

6 servings

2 pounds jumbo shrimp

1 tablespoon olive oil

1 teaspoon salt

1 teaspoon paprika

$^1/_2$ teaspoon cayenne (ground red) pepper

$^1/_2$ teaspoon freshly ground black pepper

$^1/_4$ teaspoon dried thyme leaves

$^1/_4$ teaspoon dried basil

Shell and devein the shrimp, leaving the shell on the tails. Rinse the shrimp well.

Preheat the oven to 350° F.

Combine the shrimp and olive oil in a large bowl; toss until the shrimp are completely coated with the oil. Add the salt, paprika, cayenne, black pepper, thyme, and basil. Toss again until the shrimp are completely covered with the seasonings. Arrange the coated shrimp on an oiled cookie sheet and bake them 10 to 12 minutes or until the shrimp are just cooked through. Do not over-cook the shrimp or they will toughen.

When the shrimp are cooked, remove them from the oven and cool for several minutes, then refrigerate and serve chilled.

# Jicama Salad

6 servings

1/4 cup olive oil

1/4 cup orange juice

2 tablespoons freshly squeezed lime or lemon juice

1/2 teaspoon sugar

1/2 teaspoon salt

1/8 teaspoon freshly ground black pepper

1 cup julienned jicama

1 small green bell pepper, cut into julienne strips

1 small red bell pepper, cut into julienne strips

1 cup watercress sprigs, loosely packed

2 cups shredded Boston lettuce, loosely packed

In a large bowl, whisk together the olive oil, orange juice, lime or lemon juice, sugar, salt, and pepper until well blended.

Add the jicama, green and red peppers, and watercress to the dressing; toss to coat well. Arrange the shredded lettuce on a serving platter or 6 individual serving plates. Spoon the jicama mixture over the top and serve.

*To prepare ahead, refrigerate the dressing and vegetables separately. Toss together and arrange just before serving.*

To carry the nachos and fajitas for tailgate serving, prepare the chicken and heat the tortillas just before packing. Wrap the sliced chicken and hot tortillas separately in aluminum foil. Wrap the packets of chicken and tortillas in a thick towel or place them in an insulated carrying case. They should be used within an hour. If it is impossible to serve within an hour, chill the chicken and serve it and the tortillas cold. Pour the cheese sauce into a vacuum bottle. Reheat the black bean filling on top of the stove and place it in a wide-mouth vacuum bottle. Place the remaining cold ingredients in plastic carrying containers. Pack all of the cold things in one picnic basket or bag, and the hot things in another. Be sure to carry serving utensils and sturdy plates.

# Black Bean, Spiced Chicken, and Avocado Fajitas

### 6 servings

## Black Bean Filling

| | |
|---|---|
| ½ cup dried black beans, cleaned (see page 17) | 2 teaspoons olive oil |
| 1½ cups water | One-half 4-ounce can chopped green chilies (mild or hot to taste), drained |
| 1 teaspoon salt | |
| ¼ teaspoon crushed red pepper flakes | |
| ¼ cup finely chopped onion | 1 tablespoon freshly squeezed lime or lemon juice |
| 2 cloves garlic, coarsely chopped | |

## Spiced Chicken

| | |
|---|---|
| 4 chicken breast halves, boneless and skinless (about 6 ounces each) | 1 teaspoon chili powder |
| | ¼ teaspoon salt |

## Avocado Salsa

| | |
|---|---|
| 3 ripe Italian tomatoes, peeled | 1 tablespoon red wine vinegar |
| 1 small ripe avocado | ½ teaspoon sugar |
| ¼ cup finely chopped yellow bell pepper | ¼ teaspoon salt |
| | 4 to 6 drops Tabasco |
| 6 large flour tortillas | 1 cup sour cream or plain nonfat yogurt |
| 1½ cups (6 ounces) shredded Monterey Jack or mild cheddar cheese | ¼ cup chopped fresh cilantro (optional) |

*To make Black Bean Filling:* Several hours or a day before serving, combine the beans and the water in a small saucepan. Bring to a boil over high heat, reduce the heat to low, cover the pan, and simmer for 45 minutes. Stir in the salt and red pepper flakes and simmer until the beans are tender and all the water has been absorbed, 30 to 45 minutes longer.

Remove ³/₄ cup of the cooked beans to a small food processor or blender; puree until smooth. Sauté the onion and garlic in the olive oil in a small skillet until lightly browned; stir in the chilies. Cook, stirring, 1 minute; remove from the heat. Stir the remaining whole beans, the pureed beans, and the lime or lemon juice into the onion mixture in the skillet. Remove the black bean filling to a small bowl, cover, and refrigerate until ready to use.

*To make Spiced Chicken:* About 30 minutes before serving, preheat the oven to 400° F. Place the chicken breasts in a baking pan. Sprinkle them with chili powder and salt and bake until just cooked through, 20 to 25 minutes.

*To make Avocado Salsa:* Quarter the tomatoes and remove as many seeds as possible. Peel and quarter the avocado. Chop the tomatoes and avocado together on a cutting board to make pieces about ¹/₄ inch square. In a medium-size bowl, combine the avocado, tomatoes, and any tomato juice left from chopping. Stir in the bell pepper, vinegar, sugar, salt, and Tabasco. Spoon salsa into a serving bowl.

About 15 minutes before serving, tightly wrap tortillas in aluminum foil and bake until hot through, 10 to 15 minutes. Reheat the black bean filling. Remove the chicken from the oven, slice it diagonally, and arrange it on a platter with the tortillas. Spoon the cheese, sour cream or yogurt, and cilantro, if desired, into serving dishes.

To serve, line up the tortillas, chicken, black bean filling, avocado salsa, cheese, sour cream or yogurt, and cilantro, if desired, in that order. Let the guests serve themselves and build their own fajitas.

*It is important to prepare avocados as close to serving time as possible because they darken when exposed to the air. The addition of an acid such as lemon or lime juice or tomatoes inhibits the darkening process.*

*People seem to have strong feelings about cilantro (also called coriander or Chinese parsley). They either love it or hate it. It is usually best to have guests add it themselves if you are not sure about their tastes.*

For a tailgate buffet, pack the prepared sangria in a 2-quart vacuum bottle. Pour into a glass pitcher or directly into glasses for serving. You might want to pack a long-handled pickle fork to remove the fruit from the vacuum bottle. Pack the ice in another wide-mouth vacuum bottle. To avoid diluting the sangria, drain the excess water before adding the ice.

**FRESH FRUIT:** For a tailgate party, serve a selection of washed, seasonal, fresh fruit along with the cookies for dessert. Be sure to pack some small knives for peeling and slicing. For a fancier dessert, pack a wide-mouth vacuum bottle of our Chocolate Fondue (see page 12) for guests to dip the fruit and cookies in.

**MEXICAN COFFEE:** Make your favorite freshly ground coffee, adding 1 teaspoon of ground cinnamon to the ground coffee needed for 6 cups before brewing. To serve, add 2 tablespoons Kahlúa to each cup of coffee. If desired, place a cinnamon stick into each cup for a stirrer.

# White Sangria

About 1 quart

1 small orange
1 lime
2 tablespoons sugar
1 cup cold water
2 cups dry white wine, well chilled

1 cup white grape juice, well chilled
1/2 cup seedless green grapes or several small bunches champagne grapes, thoroughly washed and drained (optional)

Wash and thinly slice the unpeeled orange and lime on a cutting board; place the orange and lime slices and any juices left on the cutting board into a glass pitcher. Add the sugar and stir with a wooden spoon, pressing the fruit slices to release more of the juice. Add the cold water and stir until well mixed. Just before serving, stir in the wine and grape juice.

To serve, pour the sangria into 6 chilled wineglasses and spoon some of the fruit into each glass. For an attractive presentation, add green grapes or bunches of champagne grapes to the glasses before filling with sangria.

### Variation

*Nonalcoholic White Sangria:* Substitute a 6-ounce container of frozen lemonade made according to the package directions for the 2 cups wine and the 1 cup cold water. Serve as directed.

# FARMERS' MARKET MIXED GRILL

From early spring through late fall, local farmers' markets abound with fresh seasonal produce. A trip to the market usually results in a refrigerator full of wonderful fresh vegetables, fruits, and cheeses. As weekends slip into busy weekdays, however, dreams of preparing large pots of stock and exotic meals featuring the market finds fade. And so frequently when the next weekend appears, the bags of vegetables are still there, taking up space in your refrigerator. This simple seasonal grill recipe can be done with any vegetables, so buy the best of the season. While you have the grill heated, throw on the Beef or Turkey Burgers and serve them on a large platter with the vegetables. A crispy loaf of bread and a simple salad round out the menu.

Grilled
Seasonal
Vegetables

Stuffed Beef
or Turkey
Burgers

Leaf Lettuce
Salad

Farmers'
Market Goat
Cheese Bread
*(see page 152)*

Cherry
Clafoutis
*(see page 136)*

**STUFFED BEEF OR TURKEY BURG-ERS:** *Plan to make 4 burgers from each pound of ground beef or turkey. Stuffed burgers make an interesting change from the usual grill favorite. To make stuffed burgers, divide each pound of ground beef or turkey into 8 pieces. Pat each piece into a very flat 4-inch round. Top 4 of the rounds with mustard and thinly sliced pickles; top with another round of meat and pinch the edges together to make a compact burger. Grill beef burgers to your desired doneness; turkey burgers should be cooked until well done.*

**LEAF LETTUCE SALAD:** *Once you could enjoy leaf lettuce only in season and if you had your own garden. Now both green leaf lettuce and red leaf lettuce are available year-round. We selected a simple leaf lettuce salad for this menu because of the variety of vegetables already included in the Grilled Seasonal Vegetables. Pass a selection of dressings with the salad—one creamy, one Balsamic Vinaigrette (see page 69), and one slightly sweet.*

# Grilled Seasonal Vegetables

6 servings

| | |
|---|---|
| ¼ cup flavorful olive oil | 1 large zucchini, cut into 6 pieces |
| 2 teaspoons freshly squeezed lemon juice | 1 patty pan squash, cut into 6 pieces |
| 2 cloves garlic, minced | 2 medium-size red bell peppers, each cut into 3 pieces |
| ½ teaspoon salt | |
| ¼ teaspoon cracked black pepper | 6 large fresh mushrooms |
| 3 medium-size carrots, peeled, halved, and parboiled | 6 scallions, cut in half |

In a large bowl, beat together the olive oil, lemon juice, garlic, salt, and pepper. Add the vegetables to the oil mixture and toss them until well coated.

To serve, heat the coals in the grill or preheat the indoor broiler. Arrange the vegetables on 6 skewers. Brush them generously with the oil mixture and grill them until they are well browned at the edges, about 3 minutes on each side. Serve hot.

# FAST FAMILY FARE

In a hurry? This simple meal can be started early in the day and finished up in minutes at serving time. Fresh tuna is a special treat that is best when little is added to compete with its distinctive flavor. Finish up the meal with an easy butterscotch sauce spooned over the freshest berries or fruits of the season. If you wish, make a batch of Cream Puffs (see page 132) and, just before serving, fill them with the fruit and Butterscotch Sauce.

Garden Rice
Salad

Grilled
Fresh Tuna

Parmesan
Bread with
Garlic
(see page 7)

Fresh Fruit
with
Butterscotch
Sauce

*If you are using an outdoor grill, be sure to start the charcoal in plenty of time. If you are using your indoor broiler, preheat about 5 minutes before you're ready to cook.*

# Garden Rice Salad

6 servings

2  cups water

1  cup medium grain white rice

2  cloves garlic, minced

¾  teaspoon salt

¼  pound (about 1 cup) sugar snap peas or snow peas, rinsed and strings removed

¼  cup olive oil

2  tablespoons cider vinegar

½  teaspoon sugar

1½  teaspoons snipped fresh dill or ½ teaspoon dried dillweed

½  cup coarsely chopped yellow bell pepper

1  large tomato, coarsely chopped (about 1 cup)

¼  cup sliced scallions (optional)

Bring the water to a boil in a 2-quart saucepan over high heat. Add the rice, garlic, and ½ teaspoon of the salt; stir, cover, reduce the heat, and cook 15 to 20 minutes or until the liquid is absorbed and the rice is tender. Stir in the sugar snap peas or snow peas; remove the rice and peas from the heat and let stand, covered, 5 minutes.

Combine the olive oil, vinegar, sugar, dill, and the remaining ¼ teaspoon salt in a large bowl. Add the warm rice and peas, the yellow pepper, tomato, and scallions, if desired; toss to combine well. Serve slightly warm or cover and refrigerate several hours until well chilled. Stir just before serving.

# Grilled Fresh Tuna

### 6 servings

Six 6-ounce pieces fresh tuna

1/2 cup dry white wine

2 tablespoons soy sauce

1 small red onion, very thinly sliced (about 1/2 cup)

Lemon or lime wedges

Several hours before serving, rinse the tuna and pat it dry with paper towels. In a shallow nonmetal casserole, combine the wine, soy sauce, and onion. Place the tuna pieces into the mixture; turn several times to coat well on all sides. Cover tightly and refrigerate until ready to cook.

Preheat the outdoor grill or indoor broiler. Brush the grill rack or broiler pan with oil. Place the tuna on the grill or under the broiler and cook until it's well browned on one side; turn and grill until it's browned on the second side and the center has just turned opaque, about 8 minutes in all. Serve immediately with lemon or lime wedges.

*A rule of thumb for how long to cook fish is 8 minutes on high heat per each inch of thickness. This was formerly 10 minutes per inch, but many kinds of fish are overcooked and dry if cooked for that time.*

# Fresh Fruit with Butterscotch Sauce

6 servings

## Butterscotch Sauce

3/4 cup firmly packed light brown sugar

3 tablespoons half-and-half

1 1/2 tablespoons light corn syrup

1 tablespoon unsalted butter

1/2 teaspoon vanilla extract

1/2 fresh pineapple, peeled and cut into bite-size pieces

18 strawberries, hulls and stems removed

2 kiwifruit, peeled and sliced

*To make Butterscotch Sauce:* **Combine the brown sugar, half-and-half, corn syrup, and butter in a 1-quart saucepan. Bring the mixture to a boil over medium heat, stirring constantly until smooth. Stir in the vanilla and set aside for 5 minutes to cool slightly.**

Arrange the pineapple, strawberries, and kiwifruit on a rimmed serving plate or 6 individual serving plates. Stir the warm butterscotch sauce and spoon it over the fruit. Serve immediately, or the sweet sauce causes the fruit to lose moisture and the dessert becomes runny.

### Variation

The Chocolate Sauce on page 12 is also good served over this assortment of fresh fruit. For a larger group, you may want to make both chocolate and butterscotch sauces and drizzle a little of both over each serving.

# GREEK ISLAND PICNIC

Whether picnicking, tailgating, or barbecuing at home, this Greek-style portable menu works well. If you don't have a grill that you can carry, or access to one, grill the meat up to an hour ahead of time, wrap in foil, overwrap in newspapers, and pack into the car. If you eat within an hour, the meat should still be warm when you're ready to enjoy it. Just slightly undercook it, since the meat will continue to cook when wrapped in the foil.

As with any picnic away from home, be sure to have everything you need in the picnic basket. And if the weather isn't conducive to an outdoor outing, have it indoors. Push aside some furniture, spread out a blanket, and serve up the meal.

Tzaziki

Souvlaki
in Pita

Greek Salad

Butter Cookies
*(see page 126)*

 *Simple to make, low in calories, and refreshingly addicting!*

 *Serve with a loaf of crusty bread or as a topping for souvlaki.*

### SAFETY TIP

*To keep your food from spoiling, hot food should be kept hot and cold food cold. Never leave perishable foods unrefrigerated more than 2 hours.*

### GENERAL PICNIC CHECKLIST

- **A** *ground cover (beach towels, straw mat, old comforter)*
- **C**harcoal, matches, grill (if barbecuing)
- **F**irst-aid kit, insect repellent, sunscreen
- **L**inen or paper napkins
- **O**peners (corkscrew, can opener, bottle opener)
- **P**aper plates, cups
- **P**lastic bags (for disposing refuse)
- **S**erving utensils and cutting board
- **S**ilverware: forks, knives, spoons
- **V**olleyball, Frisbee, baseball and bat
- **W**ater or damp cloth for cleanup

## Tzaziki

4 to 6 servings

1 cup plain nonfat yogurt
1 large cucumber, peeled, seeded, and shredded

Salt to taste
2 cloves garlic, mashed to a paste

Place the yogurt in a strainer lined with cheesecloth or a coffee filter and put in the refrigerator for 1 to 6 hours in order to drain off the liquid. The longer yogurt drains, the thicker it becomes.

Sprinkle the cucumber with salt and let it stand in a strainer for about 10 minutes. Squeeze out the excess moisture with your hands, then combine the cucumber with the yogurt and garlic. Taste, add more salt if desired, and refrigerate for an hour or more before serving.

## Souvlaki in Pita

6 servings

### Marinade

¼ cup olive oil
2 tablespoons freshly squeezed lemon juice
2 tablespoons red wine vinegar

2 tablespoons dried oregano leaves
Salt and freshly ground black pepper to taste

2 pounds boneless leg of lamb, cut into 1-inch cubes

6 pita breads

*To make Marinade:* Combine the oil, lemon juice, vinegar, oregano, salt, and pepper. Pour the marinade over the lamb. Let stand at room temperature for 1 hour or overnight in the refrigerator.

Thread the lamb onto skewers. Grill over hot coals or broil in the oven for 5 minutes on each side, turning once. Serve in pita pockets along with Tzaziki (see page 52).

## Greek Salad

6 servings

### Dressing

6 tablespoons olive oil

3 tablespoons freshly squeezed lemon juice

1 clove garlic, peeled and crushed

1½ teaspoons dried oregano leaves

½ teaspoon salt

Freshly ground black pepper to taste

3 cups mixed salad greens trimmed, rinsed, and torn into bite-size pieces

2 large ripe tomatoes, cut into eighths

1 small red onion, thinly sliced (about ½ cup)

1 medium-size green bell pepper, cored, seeded, and cut into chunks (about ¾ cup)

⅓ cup imported black olives (kalamata preferred)

½ cup feta cheese, crumbled

*To make Dressing:* Blend together the oil, lemon juice, garlic, oregano, salt, and pepper. Remove and discard the garlic before dressing the salad.

Toss the salad greens, tomatoes, onion, and bell pepper in a salad bowl. Just before serving, add the olives and cheese. Dress the salad. Serve immediately.

To prevent the wood from burning when using wooden skewers, soak them in water for 30 minutes before threading the food onto the skewers.

The crushed whole garlic clove lightly infuses the dressing with flavor. Be sure to remove and discard it before dressing the salad.

To crush a clove of garlic, position the flat side of a knife against the clove and firmly press against it with the palm of your hand.

To make ahead, combine the dressing ingredients and refrigerate. Trim, rinse, and dry the greens, wrap in a linen towel or paper towels, and refrigerate for up to 2 days before using.

# SATURDAY EVENING

Saturday evening falls smack in the middle of every weekend, making it the easiest occasion to do the most time-consuming entertaining. There's enough time to shop, cook, and to have a long leisurely meal with family and friends. One Saturday, invite some friends along with their children. Make a hearty soup, crisp salad, and heavenly dessert for all, but turn a basic dough into a pizza for the young set and into Focaccia for the grown-ups.

Consider having an international wine festival. Make a multi-course meal and sample wines from different countries with each course. Every once in a while, give a formal dinner. Set the table with your best of everything—linen, china, crystal, silver, if you have them—invite some good friends, and enjoy a fabulous evening of food and conversation.

Even those without a sweet tooth enjoy dessert. One Saturday, set out a dessert table, brew some rich flavorful coffee, and have a crowd in to sample goodies from Crêpes Suzette to Cream Puffs, with cheesecake and pies in between.

Tuscan Bean
Soup

Fried Dough
Pizzas, Pizza,
or
Focaccia

Caesar-Style
Salad

Chocolate
Berry Tart
*(see page 142)*

# COUNTRY ITALIAN

Some Saturday evenings, it's fun to invite not only your friends to dinner, but also their children. At these times, you need a versatile menu that works well for all ages. The adults, and perhaps some of the kids, will like the bean soup. Serve Focaccia—a baked breadlike dough—with the soup for the adults; and make either Fried Dough Pizzas or a regular one topped with sauce, cheese, and a selection of toppings for the children. Or there's nothing wrong with serving the pizza to all.

Serve dinner to the kids in the game room—let them eat at their own pace while playing Nintendo, Monopoly, or cards. Set a table with glasses, napkins, plates, the salad, and an ice bucket filled with a selection of juices. Set the grown-ups' table within earshot of the kids but far enough away for them to enjoy their own conversation. You might keep Pictionary, Scrabble, or Trivial Pursuit nearby, just in case your guests are game lovers.

Set the coffee, milk, and tea along with the dessert in the kitchen and let the guests help themselves.

# Tuscan Bean Soup

6 servings

1 cup dried cannellini or other white beans

1 medium-size onion, finely chopped (about 1 cup)

2 tablespoons olive oil

2 ribs celery, finely chopped (about 1⅓ cups)

2 large carrots, finely chopped (about 1½ cups)

2 cloves garlic, minced

1 medium-size ripe tomato, peeled, seeded, and diced, or 1 cup canned crushed tomatoes

4 cups water

1½ teaspoons salt or to taste

Freshly ground black pepper to taste

2 cups thinly sliced savoy or other green cabbage

¼ cup minced fresh Italian (flatleaf) parsley

Freshly grated Parmesan cheese

Sort through the beans and discard any stones, pebbles, or broken beans. Soak overnight (or use the quick-soak method; see sidebar), then drain.

Sauté the onion in the olive oil in a large saucepan over medium-high heat until golden, 5 to 10 minutes. Add the celery, carrots, and garlic, and sauté an additional 5 minutes. Add the tomato, water, and soaked beans. Bring to a boil over high heat, reduce the heat to low, cover, and simmer for 1 hour.

Puree about half to two-thirds of the soup in a blender or food processor and return to the saucepan. Bring to a boil over high heat, add the salt, pepper, cabbage, and parsley, reduce the heat to low, and simmer, uncovered, for 15 minutes. Taste and adjust the seasonings. Serve hot, garnished with Parmesan.

*To serve the soup the classic way, place a piece of day-old Italian bread in the bowl before adding the soup.*

*To make ahead, prepare the soup up to the point of adding the cabbage. Refrigerate for 1 or 2 days or freeze up to 3 months.*

*Our Tuscan Bean Soup doesn't require an entire can of tomatoes. What should you do with the leftovers? Either toss the contents into the soup or make Italian-Style Tomato Sauce (see page 62) and use the sauce to make English Muffin Pizzas. Just spread the sauce on a toasted English muffin, sprinkle with grated cheese, and broil until the cheese is melted, 2 to 3 minutes.*

**QUICK-SOAK METHOD:** *If you forget to soak the beans, cover them with cold water, bring to a boil, remove from the heat, cover, and let stand for 1 hour to rehydrate them. Then, proceed with the recipe.*

## Basic Dough

Enough dough for one 12- to 14-inch Focaccia, 6 to 8 Fried
Dough Pizzas, or one 12- to 14-inch Pizza

The dough takes a matter of
minutes to prepare in the food
processor.

If time is short, use fast-rising yeast,
following package directions.

To make ahead, prepare the
dough in the morning and
place it, covered, in the refrigerator to
rise. It will be ready by dinner. Bring
to room temperature before continuing
with recipe.

3/4 cup warm water (105°
to 115° F)

1 package active dry
yeast

1 teaspoon sugar
(optional)

2¼ cups all-purpose flour

1 teaspoon salt

1 tablespoon olive or
vegetable oil

Combine the water, yeast, and sugar, if desired, in a small bowl.
Let stand 10 minutes to proof the yeast.

*By hand:* Combine the flour and the salt in a large bowl. Stir
in the yeast mixture and the oil until a soft smooth dough forms.

*In a food processor fitted with a steel blade:* Combine the flour and
salt by pulsing twice. Blend in half the yeast mixture with a few
quick pulses. Add the rest of the yeast and the oil through the
feed tube while the machine is on, and operate until the mixture
forms a ball of dough, 30 to 45 seconds.

Turn the dough out onto a lightly floured board and knead 5
minutes, adding a bit more flour as necessary to make the dough
manageable. Shape the dough into a ball on the board and cover
it with a bowl. Let rise until double in bulk, 45 minutes to 1
hour. Punch down the dough, remove from the bowl, and knead
for 1 minute.

### Variations

*Herb:* Add either 1 teaspoon crushed dried rosemary or 1
teaspoon *each* dried oregano leaves and dried basil when adding the flour.

After punching down the dough, knead in one of the following flavorings along with some additional flour if the

dough becomes sticky. Let stand 15 to 20 minutes before using.

*Cheese:* Knead in ¼ cup freshly grated Parmesan or Romano cheese.

*Onion:* Knead in ¼ cup finely minced shallots or sweet onion, cooked in 1 teaspoon olive oil until softened, then cooled.

## Fried Dough Pizzas

### 4 to 6 servings

Oil, for frying
1 recipe Basic Dough (see page 58)

2 cups Italian-Style Tomato Sauce (see page 62), heated
Freshly grated Parmesan cheese to taste

Heat 2 inches of oil in a deep-sided frying pan to 375° F.

Divide the dough into 6 to 8 pieces and stretch each piece into an oval. Fry the dough in the hot oil until golden on both sides, about 2 minutes each side, turning once. Drain well on paper towels.

Serve the fried dough topped with about ¼ cup sauce and sprinkled with Parmesan.

*Kids love stretching the pizza dough. Let them be creative, since the dough will fry no matter what shape it's in. After you've fried the dough for them, let them top it at the table with the sauce and cheese.*

*For a thin crust, make a 14-inch pie, for a thicker, more breadlike crust, a 12-inch pie.*

*If time is short, use a good-quality jarred sauce.*

## Pizza

4 to 6 servings

Cornmeal

1 recipe Basic Dough (see page 58)

1 cup Italian-Style Tomato Sauce (see page 62)

8 ounces mozzarella, shredded (2 cups)

Sliced red bell peppers or onions (optional)

Freshly grated Parmesan cheese to taste

Preheat the oven to 450° F. Lightly oil a 12- or 14-inch round pan, then dust with cornmeal.

Stretch or roll the dough into a circle to fit the pan. Pinch the edges to form a rim. Spread the sauce over the dough, leaving a 1-inch border. Sprinkle with the mozzarella and with the peppers or onions, if desired. Add the Parmesan.

Bake until the crust is browned and the cheese bubbly, 20 to 25 minutes.

### Variations

- Top with anchovies, artichoke hearts, black olives, capers, chopped clams, green peppers, meatballs, mushrooms sautéed in butter, pepperoni, or sausages.
- For a New Haven–style white clam pizza, top the Basic Dough with diced fresh clams, lots of minced fresh garlic, and mozzarella and Parmesan.

# Focaccia

### 6 to 8 servings

Cornmeal

1 recipe Basic Dough (see page 58)

2 tablespoons olive oil

3 cloves garlic, finely slivered

Coarse salt to taste

Preheat the oven to 400° F. Lightly oil a 12- or 14-inch round pan or a baking sheet, then dust with cornmeal.

Press or stretch the dough into a circle on the pan. Brush the dough with the oil and press the garlic into the dough with your fingertips. Sprinkle with salt. Let the dough rise for 15 to 20 minutes before baking.

Bake until golden, 25 to 35 minutes for the 12-inch loaf, 20 to 25 for the 14-inch.

### Variations

*Onion:* Add ½ cup thinly sliced onions in place of or in addition to the garlic.

*Plain:* Omit the garlic.

*Fennel:* Add 1 to 2 teaspoons fennel seeds in place of or in addition to the garlic.

*Herb:* Add 1 teaspoon dried basil.

*For thin, crisp Focaccia, use the 14-inch pan; for more breadlike, thicker Foccacia, use the 12-inch pan. Or, shape the dough as desired on a baking sheet.*

*For an easier version, use freshly made dough from the supermarket or local pizzeria.*

⊞ *To make ahead, prepare completely and refrigerate for a day or two. Or, freeze 1-cup portions and use as needed.*

# Italian-Style Tomato Sauce

### About 3 cups

2 medium-size onions, chopped (about 2 cups)

2 cloves garlic, minced

1 tablespoon olive oil

One 28-ounce can crushed tomatoes in puree

2 teaspoons dried oregano leaves

1 teaspoon dried basil

1 bay leaf

Salt and freshly ground black pepper to taste

Sauté the onions and garlic in the oil in a heavy saucepan over medium-high heat until the onions are soft, about 5 minutes. Mix in the remaining ingredients. Simmer the sauce over very low heat, uncovered, until thickened, 30 to 45 minutes. Remove and discard the bay leaf. Taste and adjust the seasonings.

# Caesar-Style Salad

### 6 servings

## Garlic Croutons

2 tablespoons olive oil

2 tablespoons unsalted butter

3 cloves garlic, crushed

4 to 5 slices day-old bread, crusts trimmed, then cubed

## Dressing

¼ cup olive oil

Juice from 1 lemon

1 clove garlic, finely minced

Salt and freshly ground black pepper to taste

1 head romaine, rinsed and dried

One 2-ounce can anchovies, drained and chopped

½ cup shaved Parmesan cheese

1 cup Garlic Croutons

*To make Garlic Croutons:* Heat half the oil and butter in a small skillet over medium heat until the butter melts, about 2 minutes. Add the garlic and sauté until golden, about 2 minutes. Add enough bread cubes to cover the bottom of the pan and sauté until golden and crisp, about 2 minutes. Drain on paper towels. Add the remaining oil and butter to the skillet and sauté the remaining bread cubes.

*To make Dressing:* Combine the oil, lemon juice, garlic, salt, and pepper.

Tear the romaine into bite-size pieces and place in a large salad bowl. Add the dressing to the salad bowl and toss until the leaves are coated. Add the anchovies, Parmesan, and croutons. Toss and serve.

*Our version of this classic salad is made without the traditional raw or coddled egg.*

*To prepare ahead, make the dressing and refrigerate until just before serving. Prepare the romaine, wrap in a linen towel, and refrigerate until just before serving. The croutons should be stored in an airtight container for a few days or frozen. Reheat in a 425 °F oven to recrisp.*

*Smoked Salmon*
*with Avocado*

*German Wines*
Mosel Riesling Kabinett (white)
Rheingau Riesling Halbtrocken
(dry white)

*Chicken with*
*Wild*
*Mushrooms*

*Calico*
*(Wild and Brown)*
*Rice*

*Confetti*
*Green Beans*

*French Wines*
Alsatian Pinot Blanc (white)
Alsatian Minervois (country red)
Alsatian Pays d'Auc (country white)
*(continued)*

# INTERNATIONAL WINE FESTIVAL

For an evening overflowing with good conversation, invite some friends to a wine tasting. That is, prepare a number of different courses—say four or five—and have two different wines to sample with each course. Invite four or five couples and ask each couple to bring two bottles of wine. To have the matching go well, either provide them with names of suggested wines or tell them about the foods you'd like to match.

Set the table with your finest china, and provide two glasses per person per course. Try to include different shaped wineglasses. If you don't own enough glasses, do what's done at authentic wine tastings: Provide a pitcher of ice water and an empty ice bucket to let guests rinse out and reuse their glasses.

# Smoked Salmon with Avocado

6 servings

6 slices day-old bread, crusts removed and cut into triangles

Olive oil

6 ounces thinly sliced smoked salmon

1 avocado, peeled, pitted, thinly sliced, and dipped in lemon juice

¼ cup finely minced red onion

2 tablespoons capers, drained

Lemon wedges, for garnish

Preheat the oven to 300 ° F.

Brush the bread shapes on both sides with olive oil. Place on an ungreased baking sheet. Bake until evenly browned, turning once, about 20 minutes.

Attractively arrange salmon and avocado slices on each dinner plate. Sprinkle with onion and capers. Garnish with a lemon wedge and 1 or 2 toast shapes, depending on their size.

## Variations

- Omit the avocado, and instead use thinly sliced tomatoes and/or cucumbers.
- Substitute black bread for the toast shapes.

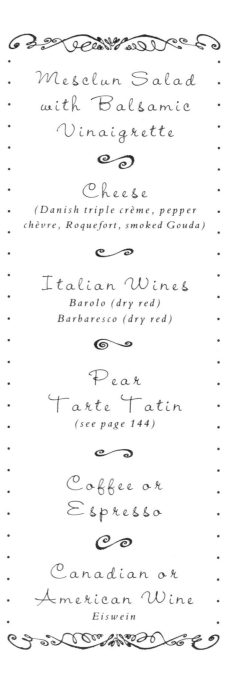

Mesclun Salad with Balsamic Vinaigrette

Cheese
(Danish triple crème, pepper chèvre, Roquefort, smoked Gouda)

Italian Wines
Barolo (dry red)
Barbaresco (dry red)

Pear Tarte Tatin
(see page 144)

Coffee or Espresso

Canadian or American Wine
Eiswein

To make ahead, cool the mushrooms in the baking dish before
adding the chicken. Refrigerate. Bring
to room temperature (about 20 minutes)
before proceeding with the recipe.

*If you want to serve a marinade that was used for raw meats or poultry as a sauce, be sure to cook it thoroughly—at least for 20 minutes. Never use the marinade without cooking it; it can contain harmful bacteria that can cause food poisoning. Cooking destroys these bacteria.*

*Use a clean plastic bag as a container for marinating meat or poultry. Not only will you need less marinade because more of the liquid will be in contact with the surface area of the meat, but you will have no container to clean.*

# Chicken with Wild Mushrooms

6 servings

1 ounce dried chanterelle, oyster, or morel
mushrooms, rinsed well

## Marinade

¼ cup olive oil
2 cloves garlic, peeled
2 tablespoons minced
    fresh parsley

Salt and freshly ground
    black pepper to taste

6 chicken breast halves,
    boneless and skinless
    (about 6 ounces each)
3 tablespoons unsalted
    butter
3 large shallots, minced
    (about ½ cup)
1 clove garlic, minced
¾ pound fresh chante-
    relle, oyster, and/or
    morel mushrooms,
    rinsed, trimmed, and
    sliced

¾ pound cultivated
    mushrooms, rinsed,
    trimmed, and sliced
2 tablespoons dry
    vermouth
¼ cup heavy cream
Minced fresh parsley, for
    garnish

Cover the dried mushrooms with boiling water and let stand until softened, 1 to 4 hours, depending on the variety of mushroom. (Each package of dried mushrooms indicates how long you should soak that particular variety.)

*To make Marinade:* Combine the olive oil, garlic, parsley, salt, and pepper in a bowl or plastic bag.

Add the chicken and let it marinate for 1 hour at room temperature or overnight in the refrigerator.

Heat the butter over medium heat in a large skillet. Add and sauté the shallots until softened, 3 to 5 minutes. Add the garlic and sauté an additional minute.

Drain the dried mushrooms, reserving the liquid, and add them to the skillet along with the other mushrooms. Sauté until the mushrooms release their liquid and the liquid is cooked off, 5 to 10 minutes. Add ½ cup of the reserved liquid, vermouth, and cream, and cook until slightly thickened, about 10 minutes.

Preheat the oven to 325° F.

Remove the chicken from the bowl or plastic bag. Discard the marinade along with the bag. Transfer the mushroom mixture to a 9- × 9-inch baking dish, top with the chicken, cover with aluminum foil, and bake in the preheated oven until the breasts are cooked, about 20 minutes. Sprinkle with minced parsley before serving.

*For simplicity, bake the chicken in an attractive dual-purpose dish—one that goes from the oven to the table.*

*For an attractive presentation, set aside 6 slices of cooked mushroom. After placing the chicken breasts into the baking pan, top each with a cooked mushroom before covering with the foil.*

*If you have a few extra mushrooms, just toss them in.*

*Riedel, an Austrian glassware manufacturer, suggests that the shape of the glass makes a noticeable difference in the taste of wines. If you have wineglasses of several shapes, you might have guests taste the same wine in different glasses to see if they can tell a difference in flavor.*

To make ahead, refrigerate after cooking—but before seasoning—the rice. Rewarm, covered, in a 325° F oven until heated through, about 20 minutes, then season with parsley, salt, and pepper.

Eiswein *is a special wine sweet enough to enjoy as dessert. It's made from fully ripened grapes that are picked while frozen and pressed before they can thaw. Eiswein—in German—means "ice wine."*

*In a wine tasting, you'll discover that there is no perfect match—many wines go well with many foods; it's up to individual preferences.*

*Like brown or white rice, cooked wild rice freezes well.*

*A linen towel placed over the pot and under the lid will absorb the moisture from the steam given off by the rice after it is cooked. If this moisture falls back onto the rice, the grains could stick together.*

# Calico (Wild and Brown) Rice

6 to 8 servings

3½ cups Chicken Stock (see page 108) or canned broth

3 ounces (½ cup) wild rice, picked over, rinsed in cold water, and drained

1 cup long grain brown rice

¼ cup minced fresh parsley

Salt and freshly ground black pepper to taste

Bring the broth to a boil in a saucepan over high heat. Add the wild rice and brown rice, stir, cover, reduce the heat to low, and cook until the wild rice grains open and the brown rice is tender (45 to 50 minutes) . Remove from the heat and let stand for 5 minutes with a linen towel between the pot and the lid. Season with parsley, salt, and pepper.

# Confetti Green Beans

6 servings

| | |
|---|---|
| 1½ pounds fresh green beans, trimmed and rinsed | 1 large red bell pepper, cored, seeded, and cut into julienne strips (about 1½ cups) |
| 2 tablespoons olive oil | |
| 3 cloves garlic, minced | Salt and freshly ground black pepper to taste |

Steam or simmer the beans just until tender, 5 to 10 minutes, depending on their size and freshness.

Heat the oil in a skillet over medium-high heat. Add the garlic and red pepper and sauté until the pepper is softened, about 5 minutes. Just before serving, add the green beans to the pan to reheat. Season with salt and pepper.

**MESCLUN SALAD WITH BALSAMIC VINAIGRETTE:** *Mesclun is a mixture of baby greens, foraged greens, fresh herbs, and edible flowers. It is available at some farmers' markets and gourmet markets already mixed; however, it may be necessary to buy the individual ingredients and mix them yourself. If you are doing that, you may want to include baby arugula, dandelion or oak leaf lettuce,* mâche *(lamb's lettuce), and a variety of herbs. Nasturtiums and nasturtium leaves make a good addition.*

*Several hours or a day before serving, rinse the mesclun well, wrap it in a linen towel, and refrigerate. To make* **Balsamic Vinaigrette,** *combine ¼ cup balsamic vinegar; ¼ cup olive oil; 1 clove garlic, crushed; 1 shallot, minced; and salt and pepper to taste. Let the dressing stand at room temperature for 1 hour or in the refrigerator overnight. Just before serving, place the mesclun in a serving bowl. Remove the garlic from the dressing; shake the dressing, drizzle some over the salad, and toss the mesclun gently until it is well coated. Serve immediately. Refrigerate the remaining dressing for use at another time.*

Mango Shrimp

Agneau
Moutarde
(Mustard
Lamb)

Roasted
Potatoes

French Peas
with
Yellow Squash

Chocolate
Profiteroles
with Raspberry
Coulis

*(see page 134)*

Instead of meeting friends at a fine restaurant for a formal dinner, invite them in for one. Using this menu, which is easily prepared ahead, allows you to be a guest at your own party. Start with cool and spicy seafood that needs only a quick sauté before serving. The mustard-coated, herb-infused leg of lamb cooks without much attention—just baste the potatoes in the pan a few times. Steam the vegetables ahead, and rewarm them as the lamb rests. Then, as you make the coffee, pull the completely made-ahead cream puffs filled with frozen yogurt from the freezer, and serve them in a pool of raspberry sauce. Your guests will want to come back to this establishment again and again.

# Mango Shrimp

About 6 to 8 servings

1 small onion, chopped (about ½ cup)

4 tablespoons (½ stick) unsalted butter

2 teaspoons curry powder or to taste (see page 17)

½ cup chopped mango chutney (Major Grey or homemade, see page 72)

3 cups cooked shrimp
Baked puff pastry shells

1 hard-cooked egg, chopped, for garnish

3 tablespoons minced fresh parsley, for garnish

Sauté the onion in the butter in a medium-size saucepan over medium heat until golden, 5 to 10 minutes. Add the curry powder and chutney; mix well. Add the shrimp and toss until heated through, about 2 minutes. Spoon into the pastry shells; sprinkle with egg and parsley. Serve immediately.

*For an attractive presentation, make scallop-shaped pastry shells. Spray natural scallop shells with nonstick vegetable spray, then press in some pastry dough (such as our Plan-Ahead Pastry, see page 140). Trim the edges and bake in a 375° F oven until golden, about 10 minutes. Gently remove from the shell.*

*To further simplify, purchase cooked shrimp, or cook the shrimp a day ahead, and refrigerate.*

*Puff pastry shells are available in the frozen-food sections of most supermarkets.*

*The remaining chutney may be refrigerated for up to one week. It is a tasty addition to cold meat and cheese sandwiches, and goes along with grilled meat.*

# Mango Chutney

**Makes 1½ pints**

2 large mangoes,
 peeled, seeded, and
 cut into ½-inch cubes

½ cup coarsely chopped
 green bell pepper

½ cup coarsely chopped
 onion

1 cup cider vinegar

½ cup firmly packed
 light brown sugar

¼ cup preserved ginger

¼ cup dark seedless
 raisins

¾ teaspoon ground
 cinnamon

¼ teaspoon salt

¼ teaspoon ground
 allspice

In a 3-quart nonaluminum saucepan, combine the mangoes, bell pepper, onion, vinegar, sugar, ginger, raisins, cinnamon, salt, and allspice. Bring the mixture to a boil over high heat; reduce the heat to low and cook the mixture, covered, for about 10 minutes, until the chutney is thick and saucy.

Cool the chutney to room temperature; spoon it into a serving dish or glass jar and serve or refrigerate until ready to use.

# Agneau Moutarde (Mustard Lamb)

6 to 8 servings

## Herbal Stuffing

½ cup minced fresh parsley

½ teaspoon dried rosemary, crushed

1 clove garlic, finely minced

1 teaspoon salt

¼ teaspoon ground ginger

Freshly ground black pepper to taste

One 6-pound leg of lamb, boned

2 cloves garlic, cut into slivers

## Mustard Coating

½ cup Dijon mustard

2 tablespoons soy sauce

2 tablespoons olive oil

1 clove garlic, finely minced

1 teaspoon dried rosemary, crushed

*To make Herbal Stuffing:* Combine the ingredients.

Spread the stuffing on the lamb, then roll and tie using kitchen twine. With the tip of a sharp knife, make small incisions in the lamb and insert the garlic slivers.

*To make Mustard Coating:* Blend together the ingredients. Several hours before cooking, spread the coating on the lamb.

Preheat the oven to 350° F.

Place the prepared lamb on a rack in a roasting pan and into the oven until a meat thermometer registers 145° F for rare, 1¾ to 2 hours. Remove from the oven and let sit 20 minutes to rest before slicing.

*This lamb is filled with flavorful herbs and topped with piquant mustard.*

*Ask the butcher for the lamb bones and use them for making a lamb stock. Use the stock for a Scotch broth or any soup or stew made with lamb.*

*Take the herbal stuffing with you when purchasing the lamb. Ask the butcher to spread the stuffing over the cavity of the lamb after boning it, before tying it with twine.*

*Be sure to let the roasted meat rest before slicing it. During the resting period the roast continues to cook, and the juices get a chance to redistribute and settle throughout the meat, resulting in a juicier, easier-to-slice roast.*

*The cooking time for the vegetables depends on their freshness.*

*To make ahead, steam the vegetables, cool under cold running water, drain well, and toss together. Refrigerate covered. Reheat in the butter just before serving.*

*Or, in a microwave-safe bowl melt the butter, combine with the savory, salt, and pepper, and toss with the cooled vegetables. Refrigerate. When you are ready to serve, microwave the vegetables on medium-high until warmed through, about 5 minutes.*

# Roasted Potatoes

6 servings

6 baking potatoes
(about 6 ounces each)

3 tablespoons vegetable
oil

Salt and freshly ground
black pepper to taste

Peel the potatoes and cut them into large chunks. Place the potatoes in the bottom of the pan to be used for the lamb. Add the oil; toss to coat. Season with salt and pepper. Baste with the drippings and the oil 3 or 4 times while the lamb roasts.

# French Peas with Yellow Squash

6 servings

1 cup fresh peas

3 small yellow squash,
cut into 1-inch
chunks

2 tablespoons unsalted
butter

1/2 teaspoon dried savory

Salt and freshly ground
white pepper to taste

Steam the peas until tender, 5 to 10 minutes. Steam the squash until tender, 5 to 10 minutes.

Sauté the peas and squash in the butter in a large skillet over medium heat until warmed through and coated with the butter. Season with the savory, salt, and pepper. Serve hot.

# DESSERT TASTING

dessert tasting is an informal way to entertain just a few friends or to host a neighborhood get-together for a larger crowd. Select a number of different desserts from "The Weekend Bakeshop" chapter (see page 119), and prepare them early in the day, or even the night before. We have chosen some that we think will please a wide variety of tastes. Whatever your selection, include a Fresh Fruit Sampler, a platter of fresh fruit cut into easy-to-serve pieces for those who are dieting and can resist the tempting array of sweeter desserts. Provide pots of a special coffee, both decaf and regular, and a selection of teas. Champagne or a semisweet dessert wine is a nice addition but the desserts are the stars.

Chocolate
Cheesecake
*(see page 120)*

Crêpes Suzette
*(see page 131)*

Chocolate
Berry
Tart
*(see page 142)*

Pecan Pie
*(see page 145)*

Fresh Fruit
Sampler

# SUNDAY MORNING

Savor Sunday mornings—the commencement of the work-week is still one day away. Spend some early daylight time stretched out on the couch with a pile of Sunday papers and a cup of freshly brewed coffee. The first meal of the day can be a leisurely family one, with Dad and the kids cooking in the kitchen. Or you can entertain guests. One Sunday invite some close friends to relax with you, make some special French toast, filled with smoked salmon and cream cheese, and a luscious dessert. For a more casually elegant meal, serve a variation of a traditional New Orleans brunch: Cheese Grits with Chicken Grillades, Pecan Biscuits, and at the end, flaming coffee—Café Brûlot.

Instead of entertaining on Saturday evening, have guests in for a special Sunday morning brunch. As you would in the evening, set the table with linens, china, and flowers. The main difference is the meal is unhurried, informal, and, one hopes, has the sun shining through the bay window. For a sensational make-ahead meal, serve a Tarragon-Scented Soufflé Roll with accompaniments. What a special way to savor the last morning of the weekend.

# E L E G A N T   B R U N C H

## Menu

Mimosas

❧

Tarragon-
Scented
Soufflé Roll

❧

Romaine
with Cucumber
Chutney

❧

Fresh Fruit

❧

Sticky Buns
*(see page 160)*

Preparing meals ahead makes entertaining more enjoyable for the hosts. For this brunch, most of the work can be done early in the morning before the guests arrive or on the evening before. Set the table before you go to sleep. When you awaken, just put the finishing touches on the meal and brew a pot of coffee. When your guests arrive, serve Mimosas, then sit down, relax, and enjoy your company before warming the soufflé and serving the salad. Sunday meals should be leisurely.

## Tarragon-Scented Soufflé Roll

❧

6 to 8 servings

### Filling

3 cups sliced mush-
rooms (about ½
pound)

2 tablespoons unsalted
butter

2 tablespoons dry white
wine

½ cup chopped
tomatoes

2 teaspoons dried
tarragon

Salt and freshly ground
black pepper to taste

## Soufflé

| | |
|---|---|
| 4 tablespoons (1/2 stick) unsalted butter | Freshly ground white pepper to taste |
| 1/3 cup all-purpose flour | 6 eggs, separated |
| 1 3/4 cups scalded milk | 1/2 cup freshly grated Parmesan cheese |
| 1/4 teaspoon salt | |

1/4 cup minced fresh parsley

*To make Filling:* Sauté the mushrooms in the butter in a large skillet over medium heat until the mushrooms give off their liquid, about 5 minutes. Add the wine and cook until most of the liquid has evaporated. Add the tomatoes, tarragon, salt, and pepper. Cook over low heat until the liquid has evaporated. Set aside to cool completely.

Preheat the oven to 400° F. Place the rack in the center of the oven. Line an 11- × 15-inch jelly roll pan with wax paper. Grease and flour the paper.

*To make Soufflé:* Melt the butter in a heavy saucepan over medium heat. Using a wire whisk, stir in the flour until the roux is golden, about 2 minutes. Whisk in the hot milk until smooth, then simmer, stirring constantly, until the mixture thickens, about 2 minutes. Season with salt and pepper. Add the egg yolks to the sauce, one at a time, mixing well after each addition.

Beat the egg whites until stiff but not dry. Stir a few dollops of the whites thoroughly into the sauce, then carefully fold in the remaining whites. Fold in 1/4 cup Parmesan.

Carefully and evenly spread the soufflé mixture into the pan. Sprinkle with the remaining 1/4 cup Parmesan. Bake until puffed and brown, not dried out, 15 to 20 minutes. Remove from the oven. Sprinkle with the parsley. Lay a piece of wax paper, larger than the pan, over the pan, place a baking sheet on the wax paper, and invert. Remove the jelly roll pan and very carefully peel off the paper. Trim away and discard the dry edges. Spread with the filling and gently roll from the short end.

Slice before serving. Serve warm or at room temperature.

**MIMOSAS:** *Partially fill the fluted glasses with orange juice, fill to the rim with chilled champagne, and add a splash of orange-flavored liqueur.*

*If you prepare the soufflé ahead, spray aluminum foil with a nonstick vegetable spray and wrap it around the soufflé roll. Refrigerate. Warm the soufflé in a 350° F oven for 10 to 15 minutes. Slice and serve warm or at room temperature.*

*A **roux** is a cooked mixture of flour and fat that is used to thicken sauces or soups.*

**SCRAMBLED EGGS IN PEPPER CUPS:** *For a simpler entrée, fill partially cooked bell pepper cups with scrambled eggs. To make the pepper cups, slice off the stem end, then remove the seeds and membranes.*

*To scald milk, bring it to just below the boiling point. You can tell it's almost at boiling when you see small bubbles form around the edge of the pan.*

To prepare ahead, chill the salad plates, marinate the vegetables in the dressing, and prepare the romaine. Rinse it, wrap it in a linen towel, and refrigerate until just before serving.

**FRESH FRUIT:** *For a centerpiece, use a bowl overflowing with seasonal fruit.*

# Romaine with Cucumber Chutney

6 to 8 servings

2 medium-size cucumbers, peeled, seeded, and cut into small chunks (about 2 cups)

1 teaspoon coarse salt

1 medium-size yellow bell pepper, cored, seeded, and finely diced (about 1 cup)

1 medium-size red bell pepper, cored, seeded, and finely diced (about 1 cup)

⅓ cup finely chopped red onion

## Dressing

½ cup olive oil

3 tablespoons white vinegar

1½ teaspoons sugar

¾ teaspoon dried dillweed or about 1 tablespoon fresh dill

Salt and freshly ground black pepper to taste

1 medium-size head romaine, rinsed, dried, and torn into large pieces

Toss the cucumbers with the salt, let stand for 30 minutes, rinse, drain, and press out excess moisture. Combine with the bell peppers and onion.

*To make Dressing:* Combine the oil, vinegar, sugar, dillweed, salt, and pepper. Pour the dressing over the vegetables, toss well, and let marinate at room temperature for at least 1 hour.

Line chilled salad plates with the romaine. Portion the vegetables over the romaine and serve.

# DAD'S IN THE KITCHEN

Weekend mornings are often Dad's time in the kitchen. An admiring audience awaits Dad's signature dish and looks forward to this weekly occasion as a special treat. This menu allows everyone to be creative and produce a breakfast that is as exciting to look at as it is to eat.

*Designer Waffles with Assorted Toppings*

*Canadian Bacon Curls*

*Orange Juice Coolers*

**CANADIAN BACON CURLS:** *Cook bacon in a skillet until well browned on both sides. Remove from the skillet and roll into tube-shaped curls. Place on the serving platter, open side down. If the curl tends to open, place a spatula on top of it until it has cooled slightly in its curled shape.*

**ORANGE JUICE COOLERS:** *Place chilled orange juice and white grape juice in a blender. Whip until very frothy. Pour into glasses. If you wish, thread some green grapes and orange slices on a cocktail stirrer and place in the cooler.*

*Because of recent problems with salmonella and eggs, we suggest that eggs always be stored in the refrigerator. When a recipe calls for eggs at room temperature, remove only the number needed and put them in a bowl of warm water for 15 to 20 minutes before using them. In order to avoid contamination from the shell, separate eggs with an egg separator, not the shell.*

# Designer Waffles with Assorted Toppings

Four 6½-inch waffles

2 cups all-purpose flour
2 teaspoons baking powder
2 teaspoons sugar
¼ teaspoon salt
2 eggs, at room temperature

4 tablespoons (½ stick) unsalted butter, melted and cooled slightly
1⅔ cups milk
Sliced apples or pears, berries, raisins, rolled oats, nuts, and seeds, for topping

Preheat your waffle iron. Combine the flour, baking powder, sugar, and salt in a large bowl. Separate the eggs, placing the whites in a small bowl. In another small bowl, combine the yolks, melted butter, and milk.

Beat the egg whites with an electric beater until they are stiff but not dry. Fold the milk mixture into the flour mixture just until they are blended. Then fold the beaten egg whites into the milk and flour mixture to make the waffle batter.

Grease the waffle iron well and spoon the required amount of batter onto the preheated iron. Arrange a selection of toppings on the waffle batter, close the waffle iron, and bake the waffle following the manufacturer's directions. Waffles are done when they are golden brown on both sides. When steam stops rising from the waffle iron, check the waffle for doneness; it is probably ready to remove. If moist fruits have been used, it will be necessary to regrease the portion of the griddle they have touched.

# BISTRO BRUNCH

Casual is the name of the game on this Sunday morning. Set your table with colorful place mats, linen, and plates, set out the Sunday papers and a pot of coffee, and relax and enjoy the morning with friends and/or family.

Invite your guests into the kitchen to chat while you put the finishing touches on the brunch. Ask if someone would mind frying the French toast. Broil the grapefruit just when the French toast is ready, then take everything to the table. Before sitting down to enjoy the meal, make sure there's plenty of hot coffee.

*Broiled
Grapefruit*

*Smoked Salmon
French Toast*

*Boston
Lettuce Salad*

*Frangipane
Tart*
*(see page 146)*

**BROILED GRAPEFRUIT:** *Slice a grapefruit in half and section it using a grapefruit knife, then proceed with one of the following:*

*Sprinkle with brown sugar and dot with butter.*

*Sprinkle with maple sugar and dot with butter.*

*Spread with honey and dot with butter.*

*Add a splash of sherry or orange-flavored liqueur, when not serving for breakfast or brunch.*

*Broil until heated through and golden, 5 to 10 minutes.*

# Smoked Salmon French Toast

4 servings

## Batter

1 cup all-purpose flour

1 teaspoon baking powder

1 teaspoon salt

One 12-ounce can beer

2 eggs, lightly beaten

2 tablespoons unsalted butter

1 medium-size onion, finely diced (about 1 cup)

¼ pound smoked salmon, chopped

One 3-ounce package cream cheese

1 tablespoon chopped fresh chives

Freshly ground black pepper to taste

8 slices challah or other egg bread

Vegetable oil, for frying

*To make Batter:* Combine the flour, baking powder, and salt in a bowl. Add the beer and eggs while stirring. Mix thoroughly, then let rest for 30 minutes.

Heat the butter over medium-high heat in a small skillet. Add the onion and cook until soft, 3 to 5 minutes. Add the smoked salmon and cook an additional minute, then remove from the skillet and combine with the cream cheese, chives, and pepper.

Spread the salmon mixture on four slices of the bread and top with the remaining bread to form sandwiches. Dip the sandwiches in the batter, then fry in oil in a large skillet over medium-high heat until golden on both sides, 1 to 2 minutes per side. Slice in half diagonally and serve.

### Variations

*Honey Toast:* Spread the challah with honey before dipping it in the batter.

*Cream Cheese 'n' Chives Toast:* Spread the challah with a mixture of cream cheese and chives before dipping it in the batter.

 *Less expensive salmon bits are fine for this recipe.*

*For a simpler make-ahead version, butter a casserole large enough to snugly fit the sandwiches and set the sandwiches in. In place of the batter, beat 4 eggs with 1/4 cup milk, pour over the sandwiches, and refrigerate overnight. In the morning, place the casserole into a preheated 425° F oven and bake until golden, 10 to 15 minutes. Slice in half and serve.*

*Keep the cooked toast warm on a serving platter in a very low oven while frying the remaining slices.*

**BOSTON LETTUCE SALAD:** *Wash and dry Boston lettuce, then dress with a favorite vinaigrette.*

Cheese Grits
with Chicken
Grillades

❧

Red Leaf
Lettuce and
Watercress
Salad

❧

Pecan
Biscuits
*(see page 157)*

❧

Peach Cobbler
*(see page 137)*

❧

Café Brûlot

# SOUTHERN SUNDAYS

Reminiscent of a leisurely New Orleans brunch, this menu features a variation of the traditional comfort food, cheese grits. Grillades, usually made of veal or beef, are often found in the company of a steaming scoop of well-buttered grits. Here, translated to chicken breasts, the grillades contribute a peppery accent to the cheese-layered grits. Just add a salad (we suggest one of red leaf lettuce and watercress), biscuits, fresh Peach Cobbler, and a bowl of New Orleans's spectacular flaming Café Brûlot.

# Cheese Grits with Chicken Grillades

4 servings

## Cheese Grits

3 cups hot cooked grits

2 cups shredded cheddar cheese (about 4 ounces)

## Chicken Grillades

3 chicken breast halves, boneless and skinless (about 6 ounces each)

$1/3$ cup all-purpose flour

$1/2$ teaspoon salt

$1/4$ teaspoon cracked black pepper

$1/4$ teaspoon dried thyme leaves

$1/8$ teaspoon cayenne (ground red) pepper

1 tablespoon unsalted butter or vegetable oil

1 small onion, chopped (about $1/2$ cup)

1 small green bell pepper, chopped (about $1/2$ cup)

1 rib celery, chopped (about $2/3$ cup)

2 cloves garlic, minced

$1 1/2$ cups Chicken Stock (see page 108), canned broth, or water

2 medium-size tomatoes, peeled and chopped

*To make Cheese Grits:* Preheat the oven to 375° F. In a well-greased $1 1/2$-quart casserole, layer half of the grits, half of the cheese, the remaining grits, and the remaining cheese. Bake the cheese grits 30 minutes, or until bubbly and heated through.

*To make Chicken Grillades:* Meanwhile, cut the chicken breasts lengthwise into $3/4$-inch-wide strips. In a pie plate, combine the flour, salt, black pepper, thyme, and cayenne. Roll the chicken strips in the flour mixture. In a large skillet, heat half of the butter or oil. Sauté the chicken strips until golden on one side, about 5

(continued)

## ALL ABOUT GRITS

*Grits used to be made from corn that had been soaked in a lye solution to remove the outer coating. Today they are produced as part of the process of making other ground-corn products. The hulls of the corn are removed by steaming, then the corn is dried and ground. The finest particles are sold as corn flour, the medium-size particles are cornmeal, and the largest ones are grits. You can get regular grits, which take the longest to cook; quick-cooking grits, which cook in 5 minutes or less; and instant grits, which are precooked and may be rehydrated with boiling water. Small mills and some health food stores sell natural grits, which are creamier in color and contain the whole corn kernel. They are usually more flavorful but do not store as well.*

**RED LEAF LETTUCE AND WATER-CRESS SALAD:** *Select the freshest greens available. Rinse and drain them, then wrap in a linen towel and chill until you're ready to toss the salad. The blandness of the leaf lettuce balances the peppery flavor of the watercress. If red is unavailable, substitute green leaf lettuce.*

 *Café Brûlot is more of a performance than a recipe. In Louisiana, they make it in special Brûlot bowls, but any chafing dish or 1-quart fondue pot with a heat source under it will do.*

minutes. Turn the chicken, add the remaining butter or oil, the onion, pepper, celery, and garlic. Sauté until the chicken is golden on the other side, about 5 minutes.

Remove the chicken to a plate. Stir any remaining flour mixture into the vegetable mixture left in the pan. Gradually stir in the stock, broth, or water and tomatoes. Cook, stirring constantly, until the mixture comes to a boil and thickens. Return the chicken to the sauce; cook over low heat until the grits are ready to serve, no longer than 15 minutes.

## Café Brûlot

4 servings

| | |
|---|---|
| 1 lemon | 2 sugar cubes |
| 1 small orange | 2 cinnamon sticks |
| 1/4 cup Grand Marnier or other orange-flavored liqueur | 12 whole cloves |
| | 2 cups hot dark coffee with chicory |
| 1/4 cup brandy | |

Peel the lemon and orange, removing the skin of each in one long spiral. Reserve the peels; use the fruit for another purpose. Push the tines of a fondue fork through the ends of the 2 peels.

In a Brûlot bowl or 1-quart chafing dish, combine the Grand Marnier or other orange-flavored liqueur, brandy, sugar cubes, cinnamon sticks, and cloves. Place the peels in the bowl, still attached to the fork. Warm the mixture over an alcohol lamp or can of Sterno until vapors rise from the bowl. Ignite the mixture and stir to keep the alcohol burning. Lift the peels using the fork; spoon the flaming liquid over the spirals of citrus peel. When the flames have subsided, gradually add the coffee, pouring it around the edges of the bowl. Stir the coffee mixture, then ladle it into cups.

Traditionally, Sunday dinner is for feasting; it is the one meal of the week when there is time to make the food as special as the folks you are cooking for. Families used to gather at Grandma's house for a nostalgic repast—all the favorites from back when Grandma was Mom and everyone was growing up together in the "home place." Today family members often live thousands of miles apart and may only get together once a year, but Sunday dinner in each household can still provide the sense of tradition and security it did in the past. The largest meal should be planned around the other events of the day with time allowed for the unhurried enjoyment of a very special meal together. For a quiet Sunday with just the family, try our special Roasted Zucchini Chicken; for an afternoon planned around the big game on television, try our hearty Alsatian Choucroute Garni. For Sunday celebrations and holidays, serve Turkey with Whole Wheat–Pecan Stuffing. For an elegant dinner, prepare our Beef Bourguignonne.

# FAMILY DINNER

Watercress
and Endive
Salad

Roasted
Zucchini
Chicken

Herbed
Noodles

Sour Cream—
Apple Pie
*(see page 148)*

ecades ago, Sunday dinners were sacrosanct; the entire, and often extended, family sat around the dinner table eating a multicourse meal while discussing whatever came to mind. Unfortunately, with our harried lives this tradition has almost been lost. Why not try to resurrect it—at least for one Sunday a month? Get the family not only to eat together, but to spend time in the kitchen preparing the meal. There are always enough tasks for everyone to do, whether setting the table, preparing the salad dressing, or making the dessert. One fun job in this dinner is stuffing the chicken. Instead of placing the zucchini stuffing in the chicken's cavity, it goes between the skin and the meat. Another job might be to slice the apples for the pie. Whatever each family member does, remember the important thing is to be together.

# Watercress and Endive Salad

8 servings

4 heads Belgian endive, sliced

2 bunches watercress, stems removed

1 pound mushrooms, cleaned and sliced

½ cup shredded Jarlsberg cheese

## Dressing

1 cup light sour cream

½ cup olive oil

2 tablespoons Dijon mustard

2 tablespoons red wine vinegar

1 clove garlic, minced

Salt and freshly ground black pepper to taste

Toss the endive, watercress, mushrooms, and cheese together in a salad bowl.

*To make Dressing:* Mix together the sour cream, oil, mustard, vinegar, garlic, salt, and pepper. Just before serving, pour the dressing over the ingredients in the salad bowl and toss.

### Variations

• Use plain yogurt instead of sour cream.
• Use Gruyère, provolone, Swiss, or other cheese instead of the Jarlsberg.

 *Instead of providing a salad with the meal, serve it as a separate course.*

*To make ahead, prepare the dressing, clean the salad greens and wrap them in a linen towel, and shred the cheese. Refrigerate each separately until ready to combine and serve. Clean the mushrooms either by wiping with a damp towel or quickly rinsing under cold water. Do not slice the mushrooms until ready to serve the salad; if sliced ahead, they will darken.*

# Roasted Zucchini Chicken

### 4 to 6 servings

2 medium-size zucchini, shredded (about 3 cups)
Salt
2 tablespoons unsalted butter
1 cup fresh bread crumbs
4 ounces low-fat ricotta cheese (about 1 cup)
3 tablespoons freshly squeezed lemon juice

2 tablespoons freshly grated Parmesan cheese
1 tablespoon minced fresh parsley
1 teaspoon *each* dried basil, tarragon, and chives
1 egg, lightly beaten
One 3½- to 4-pound chicken
1 tablespoon olive oil
Salt and freshly ground black pepper to taste

Place the zucchini in a colander, sprinkle with salt, let sit for 30 minutes, then rinse and squeeze out the excess moisture.

Melt the butter over medium-high heat in a skillet. Sauté the zucchini until wilted. Cool completely, then combine with the bread crumbs, ricotta, lemon juice, Parmesan, herbs, and egg.

Preheat the oven to 450° F.

With your hand underneath the chicken's skin, loosen it, beginning along the tail and working toward the neck. Stuff the zucchini mixture under the skin. Shape the stuffing to conform to the natural shape of the chicken.

Place the chicken in a roasting pan, brush with the oil, and season with salt and pepper. Bake for 10 minutes, then reduce the heat to 375° F and continue to bake until the juices run clear when a fork is inserted in the thickest portion of the thigh, about 50 minutes. Transfer the chicken to a heated platter and let rest 10 to 15 minutes before serving.

### Variations

- Use spinach instead of zucchini.
- Use feta cheese instead of ricotta.
- Stuff the chicken with ratatouille.

## Herbed Noodles

4 servings

| | |
|---|---|
| 8 ounces wide egg noodles | 1 teaspoon *each* dried basil, freeze-dried chives, and minced fresh parsley |
| 3 tablespoons unsalted butter | Freshly ground white or black pepper to taste |
| 2 tablespoons minced shallots | |

Cook the noodles in salted water according to the package directions, until al dente. Drain.

Melt the butter over medium heat in a large saucepan. Sauté the shallots until wilted, about 5 minutes. Toss in the noodles, herbs, and pepper. Taste and adjust the seasonings.

### Variations

- Use any favorite combination of herbs.
- Use only one herb.

*Make the noodles ahead and freeze them. Before adding the noodles to the herbed butter, set them in a colander and pour boiling water over them.*

**SESAME NOODLES:** *Sauté sesame seeds in the butter with shallots until golden, 3 to 5 minutes, before tossing with the noodles. Omit the herbs.*

Caponata

Choucroute
Garni

New Potatoes

Pumpernickel
Bread
*(see page 158)*

Seasonal
Fruit Crisp
*(see page 139)*

# HALFTIME SPREAD

Almost nothing will budge true gridiron fans from the TV set during late-afternoon Sunday football games. But come halftime, the armchair quarterbacks will be hungry. Provide a hearty one-dish meal that's ready whenever they are. Choucroute Garni—sauerkraut simmered in wine and garnished with various meats and sausages—can be started ahead of time and will not suffer in quality from keeping warm an extra half hour or so in the oven. For nibbling during the first half, surround a bowl of Caponata with some crackers or bread.

Set the buffet table with plates, napkins, and serving and eating utensils before the kickoff. Place bottles of beer and/or Alsatian Riesling (white) wines in a bucket of ice to chill. When you hear the two-minute warning, remove the Choucroute Garni from the oven and set on the buffet along with a variety of mustards, New Potatoes, and a freshly baked loaf of Pumpernickel Bread or any good-quality hearty bread. Let everyone enjoy the main meal during halftime. Wait until the final whistle to serve dessert and coffee. For a simpler dessert, serve fruit and cheese.

# Caponata

About 10 cups

½ cup olive oil

2 medium-size egg-plants, unpeeled and cut into 1-inch cubes

2 large onions, chopped (about 3 cups)

2 ribs celery, chopped (about 1⅓ cups)

2 medium-size green or red bell peppers, chopped (about 1½ cups)

2 cloves garlic, minced

2½ pounds tomatoes, peeled, seeded, and diced, or one 28-ounce can crushed tomatoes

½ cup pitted green olives, chopped

½ cup minced fresh parsley

⅓ cup red wine vinegar

¼ cup chopped pimiento

¼ cup chopped fresh basil or 2 tablespoons dried basil

2 tablespoons sugar

1 tablespoon salt or to taste

1 teaspoon freshly ground black pepper

Heat the oil in a large saucepan over medium-high heat. Add the eggplants and onions, and toss for a few minutes. Add the celery, bell peppers, and garlic, and sauté for about 5 minutes. Stir in the remaining ingredients, reduce heat to medium-low, cover, and simmer for 30 minutes. Remove the cover and simmer until thickened, about 10 minutes, depending on the juiciness of the tomatoes. Taste and adjust the seasonings. Serve at room temperature.

*When you have lots of fresh vegetables on hand from a visit to the farmers' market or supermarket, or leftover from cooking, toss and simmer them together with some herbs and other flavorings to make a go-with-almost-anything appetizer.*

*Caponata is simple to prepare. Just toss the vegetables into the saucepan as you chop them.*

*Great to have on hand for a quick appetizer. Serve along with crusty bread or crisp crackers.*

*Store in the refrigerator for 4 days or the freezer for 3 months.*

*Choucroute Garni raises humble kraut from the hot dog sidekick to gastronomic heights. Serve along with a variety of mustards from Dijon to Düsseldorf.*

Choucroute *is the French word for "sauerkraut."*

*Like many other peasant dishes, Choucroute Garni was one of the original one-pot meals; whatever was on hand—mainly meats and vegetables—was tossed into the cooking vessel.*

*A hearty dish, such as Choucroute Garni, needs a hearty bread, such as pumpernickel, to stand up to it.*

*To make ahead, cook the sauerkraut, cool, and refrigerate. Just add the smoked pork and sausages, and return to the oven.*

# Choucroute Garni

6 to 8 servings

½ pound slab bacon

1½ pounds smoked pork loin (Canadian bacon) or butt

1 pound fresh garlic sausage

1 pound sweet sausage

2 medium-size onions, sliced (about 2 cups)

2 pounds fresh sauerkraut, well rinsed and drained

2 medium-size carrots, thinly sliced (about 1 cup)

2 large tart apples, such as Granny Smith, peeled, cored, and thinly sliced

Bouquet garni (10 juniper berries, 6 peppercorns, 3 sprigs parsley, and 2 bay leaves tied in cheesecloth)

2 cups Alsatian Riesling wine

To remove some of the salt from the smoked meats, blanch the bacon, smoked pork loin or butt, and sausages by cooking in simmering water for 10 minutes. Drain.

Cut the pork loin or butt into large chunks. Slice each sausage into 6 to 12 pieces. To remove some of the fat, brown the pork loin or butt and sausages in a 4-quart Dutch oven or other flameproof casserole. Set the meats aside in the refrigerator; discard the fat.

Preheat the oven to 325° F.

Dice the bacon, then brown it in the 4-quart Dutch oven or other flameproof casserole. Add the onions and sauté until wilted, 5 to 10 minutes. Add the sauerkraut, carrots, and apples. Bury the spice packet in the sauerkraut, then add the wine and enough water to just cover. Cover and bake until all the liquid is absorbed, about 1 hour.

Bury the smoked pork in the sauerkraut, cover, and return to the oven for 1 hour. Add the sliced sausages and cook for an additional 30 minutes.

To serve, remove and discard the bouquet garni, then mound the sauerkraut on a platter with the meats and sausages.

*To remove the acidity from the sauerkraut, soak it in cold water to cover for 15 minutes, changing the water 3 times during the 15 minutes.*

*To easily remove whole spices and herbs from a dish, first tie them together in cheesecloth (called a bouquet garni).*

*If you can't find juniper berries for the bouquet garni, substitute ¼ cup gin and add along with the wine.*

**NEW POTATOES:** *New potatoes are not a variety of potato, but simply ones that come directly to the market from the field and have not been stored. They're available year round, but in limited quantities. New potatoes are thin-skinned, small, round potatoes, ideal for steaming or boiling. Use them for salads or serve simply, just steamed. For Choucroute Garni, place steamed ones around the platter.*

Roast Turkey
with
Whole Wheat—
Pecan Stuffing

Broccoli

Baked Stuffed
Potatoes

Cranberry
Waldorf Salad

Celebration
Cake
*(see page 123)*

# SUNDAY CELEBRATION

Once turkey was only for Thanksgiving and was difficult to find the rest of the year. Today fresh turkeys are available year-round. Turkey is one of the easiest meats to prepare for a crowd. Once it has been stuffed and popped into the oven, you can forget about it until serving time. This celebration menu is good for all occasions—just decorate the cake appropriately for the celebration. And, if the occasion happens to be Thanksgiving, you may want to make our Pecan Pie or Sour Cream–Apple Pie (see pages 145 and 148), rather than the cake.

## Roast Turkey with Whole Wheat— Pecan Stuffing

*8 to 10 servings*

One 8- to 10-pound fresh or thawed frozen turkey

# Whole Wheat–Pecan Stuffing

8 cups whole wheat bread cubes

½ cup coarsely chopped pecans

2 tablespoons chopped fresh parsley

1 teaspoon dried basil

1 medium-size onion, chopped (about 1 cup)

4 cloves garlic, sliced

2 tablespoons olive oil

2½ cups water

Giblet Gravy (see sidebar)

Rinse the turkey well and place it, breast side up, on a rack in a large roaster or roasting pan. Reserve the giblets.

*To make Whole Wheat–Pecan Stuffing:* In a large bowl combine the bread cubes, pecans, parsley, and basil. In a skillet, sauté the onion and garlic in 1 tablespoon of the olive oil until golden brown. Add ½ cup of the water to the skillet and stir. Pour the onion mixture over the bread cubes; toss until blended.

Preheat the oven to 325° F.

To stuff the turkey, lift the flap of skin at the front of the turkey and loosely spoon in some stuffing to fill the space. Pull the flap of skin down under the front of the turkey and tuck the wing tips under to hold it. Spoon the remaining stuffing into the body cavity. Tie the drumsticks together.

Brush the turkey skin with the remaining olive oil. Pour the remaining 2 cups water around the turkey in the roaster or roasting pan. Cover the roaster with a lid or make a tent of heavy-duty aluminum foil to cover the turkey and pinch the foil securely around the edge of the open roasting pan. Test the turkey to see if it is done after 3 to 3½ hours in a covered roaster or 3½ to 4 hours in a foil-covered pan. The turkey is done when a meat thermometer inserted into the inside thigh muscle registers 185° F. Another test for doneness is when the drumstick moves easily. The stuffing should reach an internal temperature of 165° F.

Remove the turkey to a serving platter and allow it to stand 10 minutes before carving. Serve with the stuffing and gravy.

**GIBLET GRAVY:** *Reserve and refrigerate the giblets when you prepare the turkey. Set aside liver for another use. About a half hour before the turkey is done, simmer the giblets in 2 cups of salted water in a 2-quart saucepan until they are tender. With a slotted spoon remove the giblets from the broth in the saucepan. Reserve the giblets for another use or chop them to return to the gravy. While the turkey is standing on a platter for 10 minutes, pour the hot broth into the roasting pan; stir to remove the browned bits from the pan, and then return the broth and drippings to the saucepan. Skim off as much of the fat as possible. You should have about 3 cups of broth. Return the broth to boiling. Stir 1 cup water into ½ cup all-purpose flour until smooth, and add the mixture to the simmering broth. Cook, stirring constantly, until the mixture thickens. Taste and correct seasonings. If desired, add the chopped giblets to the gravy.*

**BROCCOLI:** *To make final prepara-tion a bit faster, the broccoli can be rinsed, drained, and trimmed into flo-rets the night before or several hours before serving and stored in the refrig-erator in a plastic bag. About 20 minutes before serving time, bring a large pot of water to boiling. Add the broccoli and cook it, covered, 5 to 7 minutes. The broccoli should be crisp-tender and bright green in color.*

# Baked Stuffed Potatoes

8 servings

5 large baking potatoes (about 2 pounds)
Olive oil
1/4 cup milk, scalded
1 tablespoon unsalted butter

1 teaspoon salt
1/4 teaspoon freshly ground black pepper
4 ounces cheddar cheese, grated (about 1 cup)

Preheat the oven to 400° F.

Scrub and dry the potatoes; rub the skins with a little olive oil. Place the potatoes on the oven rack and bake for 50 to 60 minutes, or until tender. Remove the potatoes to a wire rack and let them stand until cool enough to handle—about 20 minutes.

Cut the potatoes in half horizontally to make 10 pieces. Grease a cookie sheet. Select the 8 best-looking pieces and scoop the pulp from them into a large bowl, leaving about 1/4 inch of potato pulp next to the skin. Place the potato boats you have just made onto the cookie sheet. Scoop all the pulp from the remaining 2 pieces of potato into a bowl. Add the scalded milk, butter, salt, and pepper to the potatoes. Beat with an electric beater until the mashed potatoes are smooth and fluffy. Fold in 1/2 cup of the cheese. Divide the mashed potato mixture into the potato boats on the cookie sheet. Top with the remaining cheese.

Return to the 400° F oven until the potatoes are heated through and the cheese is melted and lightly browned—15 to 20 minutes. Serve immediately.

# Cranberry Waldorf Salad

1 cup fresh or frozen cranberries

1/4 cup water

1/4 cup sugar

2 large red apples

2 large green apples

1/4 cup mayonnaise

1/4 cup plain nonfat yogurt

1 rib celery, thinly sliced crosswise (about 2/3 cup)

1/2 cup walnuts, coarsely chopped (optional)

At least several hours before serving, rinse the cranberries and remove any stems. Combine the cranberries, water, and sugar in a small saucepan. Bring to a boil over medium heat. Cook, stirring, until half the cranberries pop. Remove from the heat; pour into a large bowl and set aside to cool to room temperature, then refrigerate until cold, about 1 hour.

When the cranberries are cold, wash and core the apples (do not peel); cut into 1/2-inch cubes. Stir the mayonnaise and yogurt into the cold cranberry mixture. Add the apples and celery. If desired, add walnuts. Stir until well blended; spoon into a serving bowl and refrigerate until ready to serve.

## Beef Bourguignonne

☙

## New Potatoes
*(see page 97)*

☙

## Baby Carrots

☙

## Bibb Lettuce Salad

☙

## Pecan Pie
*(see page 145)*

# AN ELEGANT DINNER

This spectacular dinner can be prepared ahead and finished in less than a half hour before serving. The Beef Bourguignonne actually improves in flavor when refrigerated overnight. Early in the day, wash the lettuce and bake the pie. Several hours before serving, scrub the potatoes and set them aside in a saucepan of water. Peel the carrots and set them aside in another pan of water. About 20 minutes before serving time, cook the potatoes and carrots, reheat the beef, and divide the salad onto serving plates.

# Beef Bourguignonne

6 servings

2 pounds boneless beef rump or bottom round

1 tablespoon olive oil

1 tablespoon unsalted butter

½ pound small red or white onions, peeled

½ pound assorted wild mushrooms, trimmed

One 10½-ounce can condensed beef broth

1½ cups dry red Burgundy wine

¼ cup brandy

3 tablespoons all-purpose flour

½ teaspoon dried thyme leaves

¼ teaspoon freshly ground black pepper

Several hours or a day before serving, cut the meat into 1½-inch cubes. Sauté the beef cubes, half at a time, in oil and butter in a 4-quart Dutch oven or flameproof casserole. Remove the cubes to a bowl as they become well browned. When all the beef has been sautéed, add the onions and mushrooms to the Dutch oven or casserole and sauté until golden; remove to the bowl with the beef.

Preheat the oven to 350° F.

Add the beef broth and the Burgundy to the Dutch oven or casserole; bring the mixture to a boil, stirring to loosen browned bits. In a small bowl, stir the brandy into the flour until the mixture is smooth. Stir the brandy mixture into the Dutch oven or casserole and cook, stirring constantly until the sauce has thickened. Return the beef and vegetables to the Dutch oven or casserole along with the thyme and pepper; stir to combine well. Cover the Dutch oven or casserole and bake until the beef is tender, 1 to 1½ hours.

*We have not added any salt because there is salt in the beef broth. Taste the sauce and add some if you wish.*

*This is more flavorful if made the day before serving and refrigerated. Reheat over low heat, on top of the stove, just before serving.*

**BABY CARROTS:** *If baby carrots are unavailable, cut large carrots into similar-size pieces, then pare one end to a point. Or, simply use cut carrots.*

**BIBB LETTUCE SALAD:** *Follow directions for Boston Lettuce Salad (see page 85), substituting Bibb for Boston lettuce.*

# CHAPTER SEVEN

# WEEKEND DINNERS THAT MAKE WEEKDAYS EASIER

We have a time-management philosophy when it comes to cooking—especially on weekends. As long as we're spending a weekend afternoon in the kitchen cooking one meal, why not whip together some other meals to enjoy throughout the week? With our plan-ahead options, you too can do just that.

We've started with a ham, a chicken, a large bluefish, and a pot roast and turned all four not only into meals to use the day you're cooking, but also into lots of other goodies to tuck away for dinner on your busy weekday evenings. For instance, by making a large pot of chicken stock from a whole hen, you can prepare Curried Chicken Salad for Saturday's or Sunday's evening meal and Chicken Minestrone, Chopped Chicken Livers, and Chicken Tetrazzini to eat during the week. Once you begin to view cooking one meal as a step toward other meals, you're well on your way to better managing the limited time you may have in the kitchen.

*Curried*
*Chicken Salad*

*Tumbled*
*Baby Greens*

*Broiled*
*Pineapple*
*(see page 19)*

*Scones*
*(see page 157)*

*Leftover*
*Bonuses*
*Chicken Stock,*
*Chicken Minestrone,*
*Chopped Chicken Livers,*
*and Chicken Tetrazzini*

# A CHICKEN IN THE POT

When you awaken on Saturday or Sunday morning, set a pot filled with chicken, vegetables, and water on the stove. Not only will you have a pot of stock to turn into soup, you'll also have a cooked chicken to use for a meal the same day and for dinners later in the week. Package some of the stock into cup-size containers and freeze it for use whenever stock is needed. Use the rest to make Chicken Minestrone or another favorite soup. As for the luscious and juicy meat, make a dinner, such as Chicken Tetrazzini, for later in the week, and turn the rest into tonight's meal featuring Curried Chicken Salad.

For a quick light meal for your family or friends, combine some cooked chicken with fruit and nuts and season it with curry to make a delectable salad. To complete the meal, have a bowl filled to the brim with the freshest baby greens your supermarket or farmers' market has to offer, a linen-lined basket filled with warm-from-the-oven Scones, and pineapple slices awaiting finishing touches. Then just relax and enjoy the meal and your family and/or company. You deserve it—after all, you have a head start on a week's meals.

# Curried Chicken Salad

### 4 to 6 servings

1½ cups cooked chicken, cut into cubes

1 medium-size Granny Smith apple, cored and cubed

1 rib celery, chopped (about ⅔ cup)

½ pound seedless grapes, halved

¼ cup walnuts, coarsely chopped

¼ cup golden raisins

¼ cup mayonnaise

¼ cup plain nonfat yogurt

2 teaspoons freshly squeezed lime juice

2 teaspoons Curry Powder (see page 17) or to taste

2 teaspoons soy sauce

Combine the chicken, apple, celery, grapes, walnuts, raisins, mayonnaise, yogurt, lime juice, curry powder, and soy sauce in a large bowl. Toss well. Taste and adjust the seasonings. Refrigerate until ready to serve.

### Variations

- Substitute almonds, pecans, or macadamia nuts for the walnuts.
- Substitute lemon juice for the lime juice.
- Use sour cream for the yogurt.
- Add cubed water chestnuts.
- Add Mango Chutney (see page 72).

**TUMBLED BABY GREENS:** *Prepare Mesclun Salad (see page 69) without the flowers.*

### Leftover Bonuses

**CHICKEN MINESTRONE:** *Quick-soak dry beans (see page 57), then simmer in water until almost tender. Sauté chopped onions, chopped celery, sliced fennel, and minced garlic in olive oil. Add chicken stock, chopped carrots, cubed zucchini, minced fresh parsley, dried basil, dried thyme leaves, hot pepper sauce, salt, and freshly ground black pepper, and simmer. Add shredded cooked chicken, the beans, and small pasta shells. Cook until the beans and pasta are tender. Freeze for later. Reheat and serve sprinkled with freshly grated Parmesan cheese.*

**CHOPPED CHICKEN LIVERS:** *Sauté sliced onions in oil until almost caramelized. Add chicken livers and cook through. Process the onions and livers through a meat grinder, along with hard-cooked eggs. Season with salt and freshly ground black pepper.*

**CHICKEN TETRAZZINI:** *Make a white sauce by melting some butter in a saucepan and adding an equal amount of flour. Stir in some milk and season with salt, nutmeg, and cayenne (ground red) pepper. Add a splash of sherry. Enrich by adding an egg yolk, if desired, then combine with cooked pasta, diced chicken, and cooked sliced mushrooms. Turn into a buttered casserole dish and top with grated cheese. Bake in a 300°F oven until warmed through, about 25 minutes.*

**OTHER OPTIONS:** *Use leftover chicken for making chicken enchiladas, chicken croquettes, a chef's salad, or combine with mayonnaise to make chicken salad for sandwiches.*

*Every time you purchase a whole chicken, toss the liver into a container in the freezer. Once the container is full, make chopped liver. Although it's full of cholesterol, it's iron rich and fine to eat as often as your container gets full!*

# Chicken Stock

About 8 cups

One 4- to 5-pound stewing hen, well rinsed, and liver reserved for Chopped Chicken Livers (see page 107)

3 quarts cold water

4 medium-size carrots, peeled

4 ribs celery, with leaves

3 medium-size parsnips, peeled

1 large onion, halved

Bouquet garni (fresh dill sprigs, bay leaf, whole cloves, and peppercorns tied in cheesecloth)

2 teaspoons salt or to taste

Freshly ground black or white pepper to taste

Bring the chicken and the water to a boil in a large stockpot over medium heat, skimming off the particles that rise to the surface. Add the carrots, celery, parsnips, onion, and bouquet garni; cover, reduce the heat to low, and simmer for 2 hours. Season with salt and pepper. Strain the stock through cheesecloth or a fine-meshed strainer, reserving the chicken.

### Variation

*Chicken Vegetable Soup:* To use the stock as a soup, cut the vegetables and some of the chicken and return to the strained stock. Taste and adjust the seasonings. If desired, add some rice, pasta, or barley.

# BAKED HAM DINNER

Most hams are much too large for one weekend meal. But that should encourage, not discourage, you from making one for dinner, because it will leave you with lots of ham and a ham bone to turn into a variety of entrées to enjoy some other time.

Enlist the whole family to help in tonight's meal. A child could easily combine the coating for the ham, wash the salad greens, make a vinaigrette, or even prepare the apple slices. While the others are busy with their tasks, you can put the ham in the oven, put a pot of water on the stove to boil for the Sesame Noodles, make the cobbler, and set the table.

Once you remove the ham from the oven, decrease the heat to 375° F and put the Peach Cobbler in. Dessert will be warm and ready when you are.

After enjoying the Mustard-Glazed Ham dinner, toss the meaty ham bone into a pot to start some hearty pea soup or a favorite bean soup. Package and freeze some soup and save the rest for midweek. Use the diced meat to make Ham Salad for sandwiches and a special sauce for pasta. Slice some and use in sandwiches to pack for weekday lunches or for on-the-run weekend meals.

Mustard-Glazed Ham

Sautéed Cinnamon Apple Slices

Sesame Noodles
*(see page 93)*

Tossed Salad with Vinaigrette

Peach Cobbler
*(see page 137)*

Leftover Bonuses
*Pasta alla Ham and Escarole, Split Pea Soup, and Ham Salad*

# Mustard-Glazed Ham

One 3- to 5-pound ham
1 cup firmly packed
   dark brown sugar

½ cup orange juice
2 teaspoons dry
   mustard

Preheat the oven to 350° F.

Place the ham, fat side up, on a rack in a shallow roasting pan. Insert a meat thermometer into the ham so the tip is in the center, not resting on a bone, if there is one. If not precooked, bake 20 minutes per pound until the thermometer registers 160° F. Precooked hams need only to be warmed through; cook 10 minutes per pound.

Combine the sugar, orange juice, and mustard in a small bowl. Remove the ham from the oven about 15 minutes before it is done. Spread the sugar mixture over the ham and return it to the oven. Increase the temperature to 425° F and bake for about 15 minutes. Remove from the oven and let stand for 15 minutes before slicing.

*If the ham has a rind, cut it off and score the fat diagonally, ⅛ inch deep, making a diamond pattern before baking the ham.*

**SAUTÉED CINNAMON APPLE SLICES:** *Sauté in butter half an apple per person, until just tender. Sprinkle with homemade or purchased cinnamon-sugar and serve. (To make your own cinnamon-sugar, combine about ¼ teaspoon cinnamon with 1 tablespoon sugar.)*

**TOSSED SALAD WITH VINAIGRETTE:** *Mix together a variety of rinsed and well-drained lettuces. Top with chopped tomatoes, cucumbers, carrots, bell peppers, and/or mushrooms. Serve a favorite vinaigrette on the side.*

*Leftover Bonuses*

**PASTA ALLA HAM AND ESCAROLE:** *Sauté about ½ cup diced ham in olive oil with 1 minced onion and 3 minced cloves garlic. Add 3 peeled, diced tomatoes, ¼ cup minced fresh Italian (flatleaf) parsley, salt, freshly ground black pepper, and a good dash of red pepper flakes and simmer to blend the flavors, about 10 minutes. Toss in a head of escarole, well rinsed and torn into bite-size pieces, cover, and cook until the escarole wilts. Serve over 1 pound hot pasta, tossed with 1 cup freshly shaved Parmesan cheese.*

*Prepare the ham and escarole and refrigerate for up to 2 days. For a quick supper, just cook or defrost some pasta, reheat the ham and escarole, and toss together along with the Parmesan.*

**SPLIT PEA SOUP:** *Sauté diced onions, celery, carrots, and leeks in olive oil. Add picked-over and rinsed dried split peas, a ham bone, and some water. Bring to a boil, reduce the heat, cover, and simmer for 1 hour. Season with minced fresh parsley, salt, and freshly ground black pepper. Freeze and enjoy later in the week.*

**HAM SALAD:** *Dice some ham and combine it with mayonnaise, prepared white horseradish, and Dijon mustard. Use as a sandwich filling for lunch or serve over lettuce for a light dinner during the week.*

**OTHER OPTIONS:** *Use leftover ham in strata (see page 32), in a frittata (see page 22), for a ham and cheese sandwich, in a chef's salad, or in scalloped potatoes, or serve grilled for breakfast along with eggs.*

Baked
Bluefish

*Dilled
Potatoes*

*Mixed Cherry
Tomato Salad*

*Cream Puffs*
(see page 132)

*Leftover
Bonuses*

*Fish Stock, Fish Chowder,
Bluefish Salad, and Imperial
Bluefish*

# FISH PLUS

$\mathcal{M}$any times the best prices on whole fish are for the large ones that are too big for most of today's small families. It is just as easy to bake a large fish as a small one, and then you have a second meal nearly prepared. We have chosen bluefish because of its distinctive flavor. If your family prefers a more delicate flavor, the same recipes may be used for a leaner fish, such as bass. After your family or friends have enjoyed the spectacular Baked Bluefish dinner, you can remove the remaining meat from the fish and package it for freezing. Then, simmer the head, tail, and bones in lightly salted water to make the stock for a chowder.

# Baked Bluefish

### 4 servings

One large bluefish (about 3 pounds), scaled, cleaned, and gills removed

2 lemons

¼ teaspoon salt

1 tablespoon unsalted butter, melted

½ cup coarsely chopped fresh dill

Preheat the oven to 350° F.

Line a large baking pan or rimmed cookie sheet with oiled aluminum foil. Rinse and drain the fish; place it in the baking pan. Cut 1 lemon crosswise to make thin slices. Cut the center slices into quarters; set aside. Cut the remaining lemon into wedges. Squeeze the juice from the ends of the lemon over the fish and into the cavity. Sprinkle the fish with salt, inside and out, and drizzle it with the butter.

Combine the reserved sliced lemons and the chopped dill and place in the cavity of the fish.

Bake the fish for 8 minutes for each inch of thickness. It should take about 30 to 35 minutes. As you carve the fish, save all the skin and bones to make stock. Serve fish garnished with lemon wedges.

*To prepare the plan-aheads for a busy weekday evening, after dinner remove the remaining meat from the Baked Bluefish and package it in 1-cup amounts. If you have time, prepare the Fish Stock (see page 114) right away, or package the head, tail, bones, and drippings from the platter together and freeze for later.*

*Fish has a tendency to stick to whatever it is cooked in. Covering the baking pan with oiled aluminum foil makes it easier to remove the fish, and cleanup is a breeze.*

**DILLED POTATOES:** *While the fish is baking, boil some potatoes until they are just tender and then toss them with melted butter and snipped fresh dill.*

**MIXED CHERRY TOMATO SALAD:** *Purchase a variety of miniature tomatoes. Red and yellow cherry tomatoes and red and yellow miniature plum tomatoes are readily available during summer months and are now even appearing in the fancy produce section of supermarkets all year.*

## *Leftover Bonuses*

**FISH STOCK:** *Simmer the reserved fish head, tail, bones, and platter drippings in about 1 quart salted water for 30 minutes. Strain it well; cool and freeze it or use to make the Fish Chowder (following).*

**FISH CHOWDER:** *Prepare a satisfying family meal that can be easily made ahead from the leftovers of a baked fish meal. Sauté some chopped bacon in a heavy stockpot until crisp. Drain off all but 1 tablespoon bacon fat. If you wish, you can substitute 1 tablespoon olive oil for the bacon and bacon fat. Add some chopped onion and sauté it until golden. Add the stock and chopped potato. Bring the chowder to a boil and cook until the potato is tender. Stir in some of the reserved fish and, if desired, some frozen corn. Heat just to a boil and serve.*

**BLUEFISH SALAD:** *For a cool meal on a hot summer's evening, combine some of the reserved fish with your favorite salad dressing. Serve on a bed of lettuce or in a sandwich. If you wish, you can add chopped scallions, chopped fresh dill, thinly sliced carrots, sliced celery, blanched fresh peas, or even some chopped apple that has been dipped in lemon juice.*

**IMPERIAL BLUEFISH:** *To prepare an elegant weekday dinner, use the reserved fish in your favorite recipe for imperial crab, or just stir in some mayonnaise, Worcestershire sauce, finely chopped red and green bell peppers, and capers. Spoon into a baking dish or divide into individual ramekins and bake until golden and bubbly, 25 to 30 minutes at 350° F.*

# OLD-FASHIONED POT ROAST

Although this traditional family dinner has disappeared from the menu in many homes, we felt it was time to give pot roast a new look. With the new leaner beef and shorter cooking times, a smaller-than-traditional serving of this all-American favorite can still provide the nutritional benefits and old-fashioned feeling of well-being we have associated with Mom's pot roast for generations. Ghivetch, a flavorful vegetable mixture, and a salad are all you need to round out this easy-to-prepare meal. If Sour Cream–Cherry Pie seems a bit too much for dessert, substitute some fresh fruit. Plan-ahead meals made with the reserved Pot Roast are as easy as thawing and assembling. Any small pieces and remaining broth will make an excellent base for Quick Chili.

*Pot Roast*

*Ghivetch*

*Mixed Green Salad*

*Sour Cream— Cherry Pie*
(see page 148)

*Leftover Bonuses*
*Quick Chili, Hot Roast Beef Sandwiches, and Roast Beef Salad*

*To prepare the plan-aheads, slice the remaining beef and package slices in individual servings for freezing. Scraps and end pieces may be chopped to use in chili. The remaining broth can be frozen in 1-cup amounts.*

# Pot Roast

4 servings

One 3- to 4-pound bottom round or rump beef roast
1 teaspoon olive oil
¹/₂ teaspoon salt

¹/₂ teaspoon dried thyme leaves
¹/₄ teaspoon cracked black pepper
Water

Preheat the oven to 350° F.

Brown the beef roast in the olive oil in a 5-quart Dutch oven. Drain off all fat; season with salt, thyme, and pepper; and add water to cover the roast. Cover the Dutch oven and roast in the preheated oven until the meat reaches an internal temperature 10° F below the temperature necessary for the desired doneness (at this point the temperature should be 130° F for rare and 140° F for medium), 2 to 2¹/₂ hours.

When beef has reached the correct temperature, remove it from the broth, allow it to drain well, and place it on the serving platter. Cover the roast tightly with foil and allow it to stand for 10 minutes before carving. The internal temperature will rise 10° F in that time. The final temperature readings should be 140° F for rare and 150° F for medium. Slice the roast and serve it moistened with some of the broth.

# Ghivetch

*8 servings*

1 medium-size acorn squash, peeled, seeded, and diced

3 large carrots, cubed (about 2 cups)

2 ribs celery, diagonally sliced into 1/2-inch pieces (about 1 1/3 cups)

3 medium-size new potatoes, unpeeled and cubed

1 medium-size onion, thinly sliced (about 1 cup)

1 medium-size red bell pepper, cored and cut into strips (about 3/4 cup)

1 medium-size green bell pepper, cored and cut into strips (about 3/4 cup)

1/4 pound green beans, trimmed and cut into 1-inch pieces

1/2 cup frozen peas

1 cup Chicken Stock (see page 108), canned chicken broth, or beef broth

1/4 cup olive oil

3 cloves garlic, minced

1 teaspoon dried savory

1/2 teaspoon dried tarragon

1 bay leaf

Combine all the vegetables, except the peas, in a 9- × 13-inch pan.

Preheat the oven to 350° F.

Combine the broth, oil, garlic, savory, tarragon, and bay leaf in a saucepan. Bring to a boil. Pour over the vegetables, cover with foil, and bake until the vegetables are tender, about 45 minutes, tossing twice during the cooking period. Toss in the peas about 10 minutes before the vegetables should be done. Remove the bay leaf.

*To make ahead, cool the flavored liquids before pouring over the vegetables, cover, and refrigerate for up to 1 day ahead. Bring to room temperature before baking.*

**MIXED GREEN SALAD:** *Select a variety of the freshest greens available. Rinse and drain the greens, then wrap in a linen towel and chill until you're ready to toss the salad.*

## Leftover Bonuses

**QUICK CHILI:** *For a midweek supper, heat 1 cup beef broth in a 4-quart saucepan. Stir in the reserved chopped pieces of beef, one 15-ounce can stewed tomatoes, one 16-ounce can drained red kidney beans, and 2 to 3 teaspoons chili powder. Bring the mixture to a boil and simmer 10 minutes. Serve with corn chips, shredded cheddar cheese, and chopped scallions. If you have a bit more time, sauté some chopped onions and green peppers in olive oil until they are lightly browned. Stir in 1 teaspoon ground cumin, then add the mixture to the chili.*

**HOT ROAST BEEF SANDWICHES:** *These can be made 2 servings at a time from the frozen beef and broth leftover from the pot roast. Thaw 2 portions of the roast beef. Bring 1 cup of the frozen beef broth to a boil in a 1-quart saucepan. Stir 2 tablespoons water into 1 tablespoon flour in a small bowl; stir the mixture into the broth. Taste and adjust the seasonings. Dip slices of thawed, reserved beef into the beef gravy just long enough to warm them. Do not actually cook them; they will toughen. Arrange the beef slices on a slice of firm whole-grain bread on each of 2 individual plates. Top with half the gravy. Add a second slice of bread and the remaining gravy. You can vary the sandwiches by adding something to the beef filling, such as sautéed slices of zucchini or mushrooms.*

**ROAST BEEF SALAD:** *This high-energy salad can be made 1 serving at a time for nights when family members don't all come home at the same time: Thaw 1 serving of roast beef slices. Prepare your favorite mixture of salad greens and vegetables. Top with the beef slices and a vinaigrette dressing (use bottled or see ours on page 69). Toasted walnuts or sunflower seeds make a nice finish to the salad.*

The Weekend Kitchen

# THE WEEKEND BAKESHOP

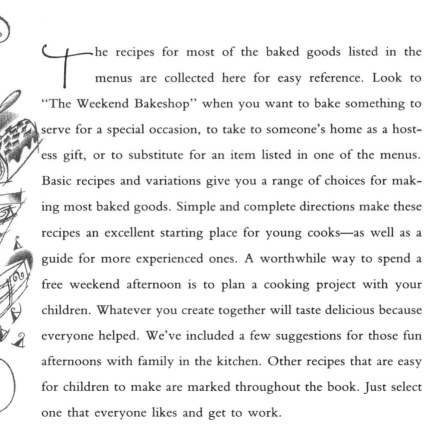

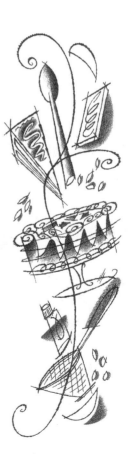

The recipes for most of the baked goods listed in the menus are collected here for easy reference. Look to "The Weekend Bakeshop" when you want to bake something to serve for a special occasion, to take to someone's home as a hostess gift, or to substitute for an item listed in one of the menus. Basic recipes and variations give you a range of choices for making most baked goods. Simple and complete directions make these recipes an excellent starting place for young cooks—as well as a guide for more experienced ones. A worthwhile way to spend a free weekend afternoon is to plan a cooking project with your children. Whatever you create together will taste delicious because everyone helped. We've included a few suggestions for those fun afternoons with family in the kitchen. Other recipes that are easy for children to make are marked throughout the book. Just select one that everyone likes and get to work.

Chocolate
Cheesecake

☙

Wild Blueberry
Cake

☙

Celebration Cake

☙

Orange
Blondies

☙

Almond
Macaroons

☙

Butter Cookies

☙

Meringue
Cookies

# CAKES AND COOKIES

**D**essert holds a special place in people's food memories. Sweet things are associated with special occasions, rewards, and the warmth of coming home to find the aroma of something wonderful baking. We have included three enticingly decadent cakes, Chocolate Cheesecake, Wild Blueberry Cake, and Celebration Cake; and four simple and simply delicious cookies, Orange Blondies, Butter Cookies, Almond Macaroons, and Meringue Cookies. Bake them for special guests or to remind your family that they are the most important people in your life.

## Chocolate Cheesecake

☙

16 to 20 servings

### Crust

One 9-ounce box choco-
late wafers, finely
crushed

Scant ¼ cup sugar
3 tablespoons unsalted
butter, melted

## Filling

Three 8-ounce packages
  cream cheese, at
  room temperature
1 cup sugar
1 tablespoon all-purpose
  flour
2 teaspoons vanilla
  extract

⅛ teaspoon salt
3 eggs
1 cup sour cream
One 12-ounce package
  semi-sweet chocolate
  chips, melted and
  cooled slightly

Whipped cream, for
  garnish

Chocolate shavings, for
  garnish

*To make Crust:* Combine the wafer crumbs with the sugar and butter. Press into the bottom and ½ inch up the sides of a 9-inch springform pan.

Preheat the oven to 350° F.

*To make Filling:* Beat the cream cheese until smooth with an electric mixer at high speed. While the mixer is running, very gradually add the sugar. Mix in the flour, vanilla, and salt; then add the eggs, one at a time, beating well after each addition. Mix in the sour cream, then the chocolate.

Pour the batter into the prepared pan and bake on the center rack of the oven for 1 hour. Remove and let cool on a wire rack. The center of the cheesecake will be soft when removed from the oven and will firm up as it cools.

For an attractive presentation, garnish with whipped cream and shaved chocolate.

*For a mess-free method of crushing the crumbs, place the chocolate wafers in a resealable plastic bag and, using a rolling pin, crush them. Add the sugar and butter, and knead in the bag.*

*Definitely not for the fat and cholesterol conscious. This sinful dessert comes from Anita Emmer of Oklahoma City, a fabulous cook who generously shared the recipe with us.*

*Easy for kids to make. With some help, even 5- or 6-year-old kids can easily prepare the cake batter. Just have all the ingredients, necessary equipment, and an adult to supervise.*

*If wild blueberries aren't available, use fresh or frozen cultivated.*

*You can make the cake 1 day ahead, cool completely, then wrap in foil.*

*Berry picking is a wonderful way to spend an afternoon with your children. In many parts of the country wild blueberries are abundant. If there is not a wild blueberry patch available in your area, try one of the domestic berry farms that have U-Pick fields. Before all the berries have been eaten out-of-hand, gather everyone in the kitchen to make our Wild Blueberry Cake. When berry season has passed, you can go apple picking and make our Apple Crisp (see page 138).*

# Wild Blueberry Cake

8 servings

2 cups all-purpose flour
1 cup sugar
4 teaspoons baking powder
Pinch salt
2 cups wild blueberries, rinsed and drained
2 eggs, lightly beaten

¼ pound (1 stick) unsalted butter, melted and cooled
¼ cup milk
1 tablespoon freshly squeezed lemon juice
1 teaspoon vanilla extract

## Crumb Topping

½ cup all-purpose flour
⅓ cup firmly packed dark brown sugar
½ teaspoon ground cinnamon

4 tablespoons (½ stick) unsalted butter, melted

Preheat the oven to 350° F. Grease a 9-inch square pan.

Stir the flour, sugar, baking powder, and salt together in a medium-size bowl. Remove 1 tablespoon of the mixture and toss with the blueberries.

Blend the eggs, butter, milk, lemon juice, and vanilla in a small bowl. Add the liquid ingredients to the dry and beat until smooth. Gently fold in the blueberries, then turn into the prepared pan.

*To make Crumb Topping:* Stir together the flour, sugar, cinnamon, and butter until crumbly. Sprinkle over the batter in the pan.

Bake until a cake tester inserted in the center comes out clean, 50 to 60 minutes. Remove to a wire rack and cool. Serve warm or at room temperature.

# Celebration Cake

12 servings

| | |
|---|---|
| 1/2 pound (2 sticks) butter, softened | 4 teaspoons baking powder |
| 1 1/2 cups sugar | 1/2 teaspoon salt |
| 4 eggs | 1 1/2 cups milk |
| 3 1/2 cups unsifted cake flour | 1 tablespoon vanilla extract |

## Frosting

| | |
|---|---|
| 5 1/2 cups confectioners' sugar | 1 teaspoon almond extract |
| 1/2 cup vegetable shortening | 1/4 teaspoon salt |
| 1/3 to 1/2 cup milk | |

Preheat the oven to 350° F. Grease and flour three 9-inch cake pans.

In a large bowl with an electric beater, beat the butter and sugar until fluffy. Beat in the eggs one at a time. Stir together the flour, baking powder, and salt; add alternately with milk and vanilla until a smooth batter is formed. Divide the batter into the 3 prepared pans.

Bake the cake layers until golden brown and a toothpick inserted in the center comes out clean, 30 to 35 minutes. Cool the cakes in the pans for 10 minutes. Loosen the edges of the cakes and turn them out onto a wire rack to cool completely.

*To make Frosting:* Beat together all the ingredients, adding as much milk as necessary, until smooth and fluffy.

To assemble, place 1 cake layer on a serving plate right side up; spread the top with a little frosting. Add another layer, upside down; spread with a little frosting. Top with the remaining cake layer, right side up. Frost the top and sides of the cake.

*For a quick and attractive presentation, arrange **edible flowers** on the top and around the base of the cake. **Edible flowers** include borage, bachelor's buttons, carnations, calendula, daisies, French marigolds, nasturtiums, pansies, roses, and snapdragons. They are available in the herb section of some markets. Do not use flowers from florists or from gardens where pesticides have been used. Beware, some flowers, such as poinsettias, daffodils, and oleander, are poisonous.*

## Orange Blondies

### 16 to 20 bars

1¼ cups all-purpose flour

1 teaspoon baking powder

½ teaspoon salt

12 tablespoons (1½ sticks) unsalted butter, at room temperature

⅔ cup firmly packed dark brown sugar

½ cup granulated sugar

1 teaspoon vanilla extract

Grated zest of 1 orange

1 tablespoon orange-flavored liqueur or orange juice concentrate

2 eggs

1½ cups semisweet chocolate chips

Preheat the oven to 350° F. Grease a 9-inch square pan.

Combine the flour, baking powder, and salt in a small bowl.

Cream together the butter and sugars using a food processor or electric mixer until light and fluffy. Mix in the vanilla, zest, and orange liqueur or orange juice. Add the eggs, one at a time, beating well after each addition. Stir in the flour mixture, then the chocolate chips.

Spread the batter into the prepared pan. Bake until a toothpick inserted in the center comes out barely moist, 30 to 35 minutes.

### Variations

- Use freshly grated lemon zest and 1 teaspoon pure lemon extract in place of the orange zest and liqueur or orange juice.
- Use white-chocolate chips in place of semisweet.
- Raisins or chopped dried apricots may be used in place of part or all of the chocolate chips.

# Almond Macaroons

1½ dozen macaroons

1 cup slivered blanched
   almonds
½ cup sugar

2 egg whites
½ teaspoon almond
   extract

Grind the almonds very finely in a blender or small food processor. Combine ground almonds, sugar, and egg whites in a small saucepan; cook the mixture over low heat, stirring constantly, until the mixture thickens and pulls away from the sides of the pan, about 5 minutes. Stir in almond extract.

Preheat the oven to 300° F. Grease 2 cookie sheets.

Drop the dough by heaping teaspoonfuls onto the cookie sheets, leaving 1 inch between the macaroons. Let stand at room temperature for 15 minutes.

Bake until golden brown on the outside and still slightly soft inside, about 20 minutes. Remove from the cookie sheets to a wire rack immediately. Cool completely; store between layers of wax paper in an airtight container.

### Variations

*Holiday Macaroons:* Top each cookie with a whole blanched almond or half of a candied cherry before baking.

*Pignoli or Pistachio Cookies:* Prepare the cookies using ¾ cup almonds and ¼ cup either pine nuts (pignolis) or pistachios. Grind the nuts together. Substitute ¼ teaspoon vanilla extract for ¼ teaspoon of the almond extract. Divide an additional ¼ cup pine nuts or pistachios among the tops of the macaroons before baking.

**TOASTED ALMONDS:** *Spread blanched almonds on an ungreased pan and bake in a preheated 350° F oven for 10 minutes or until golden.*

# Butter Cookies

6 dozen

½ pound (2 sticks) unsalted butter, softened

⅔ cup sugar

1 egg

1 teaspoon vanilla extract

1 teaspoon almond extract

2⅓ cups sifted all-purpose flour

1 cup (about 6 ounces) finely chopped unblanched or toasted blanched almonds

¼ teaspoon salt

Confectioners' sugar

In a large bowl with an electric mixer at medium speed, cream the butter, sugar, egg, and vanilla and almond extracts until light and fluffy, 3 to 5 minutes. Combine the flour, almonds, and salt, then gradually stir into the butter mixture until well blended. Shape the dough into 2 rolls, about 1½ inches in diameter. Wrap in wax paper and refrigerate until firm, about 1 hour or overnight.

Preheat the oven to 350° F. Grease 2 cookie sheets.

Slice the chilled dough into ¼-inch slices, space about 1 inch apart on the cookie sheet, and bake until lightly browned, about 10 minutes. Remove to cool on a wire rack; sprinkle with confectioners' sugar while warm.

- Melt ¼ cup semisweet chocolate chips and drizzle over cooled cookies.
- After shaping the dough into the cylinders, roll them in toasted chopped almonds, brown sugar, or date sugar. (Date sugar is made from dehydrated, finely ground dates. Unfortunately, date sugar is only available in certain parts of the country. To order by mail, contact Covalda Date Company, P.O. Box 908, Coachella, CA 92236, telephone 619-398-3551. The date sugar is available in 1- and 5-pound packages.)

*Creative Cookies:* Children love to get their hands into things. Prepare our recipe for Butter Cookies (see page 126) and chill the dough only long enough to make it manageable. Help everyone into a generous apron; then give each child a cookie sheet and a portion of the dough. Let the children grease the cookie sheets and then create flat cookie sculptures decorated with dried fruit and nuts right on the cookie sheets. Bake the cookies according to the recipe directions. If portions of the sculptures are thicker than a normal sugar cookie, it may be necessary to give them a minute or so more in the oven. Cool the cookie sculptures for at least 10 minutes before serving them with frosty glasses of milk. Children might want to make cookie sculptures as holiday presents for their friends and family.

*These cookies are so delicious, they won't last long enough to get stale. Store in an airtight container in a cool, dry place.*

*To make ahead, bake the cookies and freeze for up to 3 months. Or make the dough and refrigerate it for up to 2 days, or freeze up to 3 months. When ready to serve, just slice and bake until lightly browned.*

*It is important to use large eggs here because the volume of the white varies greatly between egg sizes, and the proportion of egg white to sugar determines the volume and stability of the meringues.*

# Meringue Cookies

**About 3 dozen bite-size cookies**

2 large egg whites, at room temperature

²/₃ cup sugar

¼ teaspoon salt

1 teaspoon vanilla extract

½ cup chopped black or English walnuts, pecans, miniature chocolate chips, raisins, dried sour cherries, chopped dates, or a mixture of nuts and dried fruit

Preheat the oven to 300° F. Generously grease 2 cookie sheets.

Beat the egg whites until fluffy with an electric beater. Very gradually beat in the sugar and salt, beating well after each addition until the mixture stands in stiff peaks. Fold in vanilla and your choice of nuts, chocolate chips, or dried fruit. Drop by teaspoonfuls onto cookie sheets to make 36 small meringues.

Bake until very lightly browned, 5 to 7 minutes. Turn off the oven and allow the meringues to stand in the cooling oven for 30 minutes longer. Remove the meringues to a wire rack to cool completely; store them in an airtight container.

The Weekend Kitchen

# OTHER DESSERTS

For a variety of classic dessert choices, consider this selection. Crêpes, Cream Puffs, Chocolate Profiteroles, Raspberry Coulis, Peach Cobbler, Apple Crisp, and Cherry Clafoutis, with many variations, give you a wide range of answers to the question, "What's for dessert?"

## A Box of Chocolates

Dipping chocolates is an easy family project, and the results provide good nibbling as well as an impressive do-it-yourself gift. Adults should oversee the melting of chocolate chips either in the microwave or in a pan of hot water. Children can assemble the foods to use for candy centers. Dried fruit, nuts, small pretzels, small cookies, and candies such as caramels and gumdrops will coat well and hold for a long time. (Fresh strawberries are also a good choice for dipping, but they must be consumed within about an hour of dipping or they will start to collect moisture.) Fondue forks and long-handled tongs are good to use for holding the item to be coated. Have children dip things into the melted chocolate one at a time and then arrange them on a wax-paper-covered cookie sheet for chilling. When all the items have been dipped, stir a mixture of dried fruit and nuts into the remaining chocolate and drop the candy by teaspoonfuls onto wax paper to make fruit-and-nut clusters. Chill all coated chocolates until firm, then place each into a candy paper and pack in gift boxes or arrange on a serving plate for the family to enjoy.

A Box of Chocolates

Crêpes

Cream Puffs

Chocolate Profiteroles with Raspberry Coulis

Cherry Clafoutis

Peach Cobbler

Apple Crisp

*Crêpes freeze very well. When preparing crêpes, double the recipe and freeze half, each separated by a double layer of wax paper. For a last-minute dessert or a quick snack, remove as many as you need, thaw them at room temperature or in a warm oven or microwave, and fill them with fresh fruit, ice cream, meat, or cheese.*

# Crêpes

### Eight 7-inch crêpes

| | |
|---|---|
| 1 cup all-purpose flour | 1¼ cups milk |
| 2 eggs | Cinnamon-sugar (optional) |
| 3 to 4 tablespoons unsalted butter, melted | |

Place the flour in a medium-size bowl; add the eggs and 2 tablespoons of the butter. Gradually add the milk, beating constantly with a wire whisk until the batter is smooth. Set the batter aside for 5 minutes; then pour it through a strainer into a 1-quart pitcher or glass measuring cup.

Place an 8- or 9-inch skillet over medium heat. When it is hot, brush it with some of the remaining melted butter. Pour in about ¼ cup batter; turn the pan so the batter forms a 7-inch round. Cook the crêpe until it is golden brown on both sides, 2 to 3 minutes on each side. Serve immediately with cinnamon-sugar, if desired, or turn out onto a wire rack to cool for later use. Continue cooking the crêpes until all of the batter has been used.

The Weekend Kitchen

*Crêpes Suzette:* In a small bowl, stir together 4 tablespoons (½ stick) unsalted butter, ¼ cup Grand Marnier or other orange-flavored liqueur, and 1 teaspoon finely grated orange zest. Spread the orange butter over the crêpes, then fold into quarters. Peel and section 2 oranges. In a skillet, heat together ½ cup orange juice, 2 tablespoons sugar, and the orange sections until the mixture comes to a boil. Place the folded crêpes in the hot syrup. Warm ¼ cup Grand Marnier or other orange-flavored liqueur in a small saucepan until you can see the vapors rising from it, then ignite with a long match and pour it over the crêpes. Serve while still aflame.

*Ham and Cheese Crêpes:* Combine 1 cup chopped Jarlsberg or Swiss cheese and 1 cup chopped ham in a bowl. Divide the mixture onto the centers of the crêpes. Fold the sides of each crêpe over the ham and cheese mixture from 4 directions to make a 3-inch square. Sauté the filled crêpes in a lightly oiled skillet until they are golden brown on both sides and the cheese has melted. Serve them with a sauce made from 1 cup sour cream or plain low-fat yogurt and 2 teaspoons prepared mustard or 1 teaspoon dried dillweed.

*The simplest dessert becomes an elegant presentation when flamed. Warm and ignite any liquor, brandy, or liqueur with at least 25 percent alcohol (50 proof) according to the directions for flaming the Crêpes Suzette and pour it over the dessert. It is best to flame the dessert on a serving cart or small table within view of but several feet away from the main table. Do not flame on a surface covered with a tablecloth.*

# Cream Puffs

8 Cream Puffs

## Dough

3/4 cup water

6 tablespoons (3/4 stick) unsalted butter

1/4 teaspoon salt

3/4 cup all-purpose flour

3 large eggs

## Vanilla Pudding

2 1/2 cups milk

1/4 cup sugar

1/4 cup cornstarch

1/8 teaspoon salt

1 egg

1 tablespoon vanilla extract

Confectioners' sugar (optional)

Preheat the oven to 400° F. Lightly grease a cookie sheet.

*To make Dough:* In a 1-quart saucepan, bring the water, butter, and salt to a boil. With the saucepan still over the heat, add the flour all at once and beat vigorously with a wooden spoon until the mixture comes away from the sides of the pan and forms a ball. Remove the pan from the heat and let it cool slightly. Add the eggs one at a time, beating between each addition until the dough is smooth and shiny.

Place the dough in a pastry tube and squeeze golf ball–size rounds onto the greased cookie sheet. Or drop the dough by heaping tablespoonfuls onto the sheet.

Bake the Cream Puffs until puffed and golden, about 30 minutes. Turn off the oven and allow the puffs to stand in the oven 15 minutes longer. Cool completely on a wire rack.

*To make Vanilla Pudding:* In a medium-size saucepan, over low heat, bring 2 cups of the milk just to boiling. Keep an eye on it so it doesn't boil over. In a small bowl, stir together the sugar,

cornstarch, and salt. Gradually beat in the remaining 1/2 cup milk and the egg until very well blended. Stir the cornstarch mixture into the boiling milk. Cook until the pudding returns to boiling; cook 1 minute, stirring constantly, until the pudding is thick. Remove from the heat and stir in the vanilla. Refrigerate, covered, until serving time.

Just before serving, split the cooled Cream Puffs crosswise and fill them with vanilla pudding. Sprinkle the tops with confectioners' sugar, if desired.

### Variations

*Cream Puffs with Chocolate Pudding:* Prepare vanilla pudding as described for the Cream Puffs, adding two 1-ounce squares unsweetened chocolate to the 2 cups milk as it heats and increasing the sugar to 1/3 cup.

*Cream Puffs with Strawberries and Ice Cream:* Fifteen minutes before serving, wash and thoroughly drain 2 pints strawberries. Set aside 8 strawberries with caps for garnish; slice enough strawberries to make 2 cups. Toss the sliced strawberries with 1 tablespoon sugar and set aside. Set out at room temperature 2 pints vanilla ice cream or frozen yogurt to soften slightly. To serve, scoop softened ice cream or frozen yogurt into the Cream Puffs, top each with about 1/4 cup strawberries, and garnish with a whole strawberry.

*Chocolate Éclairs:* Prepare Cream Puff dough as directed for chocolate dough (see page 134). Spoon out onto a cookie sheet in eight 5-inch-long strips. Bake and cool as directed for Cream Puffs. Split the éclairs and fill with either vanilla or chocolate pudding.

*Chocolate Glaze:* In a small bowl, combine 1 cup confectioners' sugar, 2 tablespoons unsweetened cocoa, and 1 to 2 teaspoons milk to make a smooth glaze. Spread over the tops of the éclairs.

# Chocolate Profiteroles with Raspberry Coulis

8 to 10 servings, about 24 to 30 profiteroles

## Chocolate Dough

¼ pound (1 stick) unsalted butter

1 cup water

1 ounce semisweet chocolate, chopped

1 cup minus 2 tablespoons all-purpose flour

4 large eggs

1 quart good-quality vanilla frozen yogurt

Raspberry Coulis (see page 135) or Chocolate Sauce (see page 12)

Preheat the oven to 400° F. Lightly grease a cookie sheet.

*To make Chocolate Dough:* In a 1-quart saucepan, bring the butter, water, and chocolate to a boil over medium heat just until the butter and chocolate are melted. Add the flour all at once and beat vigorously with a wooden spoon until the mixture comes away from the sides of the pan and forms a firm ball. Remove the pan from the heat and let the mixture cool slightly. Add the eggs, one at a time, beating between additions until the dough is smooth and shiny.

Place the dough in a pastry tube and squeeze walnut-size rounds onto the cookie sheet. Or drop by spoonfuls onto the sheet.

Bake in the preheated oven for 15 minutes; reduce the temperature to 350° F and bake until puffed, about 25 minutes. Remove from the oven, turn off oven, pierce each shell on the bottom, and return to the oven for an additional 5 minutes to dry. Remove from the oven and let cool completely before filling.

Using a serrated knife, slice each round in half, mound yogurt into one half, top with the other half, and freeze until 10 minutes before serving. Serve on a puddle of Raspberry Coulis or Chocolate Sauce.

- Use ice cream instead of yogurt.
- Serve topped with whipped cream instead of the Raspberry Coulis or Chocolate Sauce.

## Raspberry Coulis

About 1 cup

| | |
|---|---|
| One 10-ounce package frozen raspberries (in sugar), thawed | 2 teaspoons framboise (raspberry) liqueur |

Process the raspberries and the liqueur in a food processor or blender until smooth. Store in the refrigerator until ready to use. For a smooth sauce, pass the coulis through a fine-meshed strainer to remove the seeds.

**PEACH MELBA:** *Serve Raspberry Coulis over ice cream and peaches for this classic dessert.*

*Quick to make.*

*Easy for kids to make.*

*When adding flour to a processor or blender to make a batter, scrape down the sides of the container to be sure all of it is incorporated.*

*The batter puffs up during the last 15 minutes, but the clafoutis will sink slightly as it cools.*

## Cherry Clafoutis

6 servings

3 tablespoons unsalted butter

2 cups well-drained, canned dark sweet cherries or pitted fresh or frozen cherries

1 cup milk

1 cup all-purpose flour

3/4 cup granulated sugar

4 eggs

1 tablespoon kirsch or 1 teaspoon almond extract

1 teaspoon freshly grated lemon zest

1 teaspoon freshly squeezed lemon juice

Confectioners' sugar

Vanilla ice cream or frozen yogurt

Preheat the oven to 350° F.

Melt the butter in a 9-inch ovenproof dish, then pour into a blender or food processor. Add the cherries to the butter remaining in the dish and toss to coat. Set aside.

Add the milk, flour, granulated sugar, eggs, kirsch or almond extract, lemon zest, and lemon juice to the butter in the blender or processor. Process until smooth. Pour over the cherries. Bake, uncovered, until well puffed and lightly browned (a knife inserted in the center should come out clean), about 45 minutes.

Let stand 10 minutes, then serve warm, sprinkled with confectioners' sugar and topped with ice cream or yogurt.

# Peach Cobbler

6 servings

5 cups sliced fresh
  peaches
1/3 cup sugar
1 cup all-purpose flour
1 tablespoon freshly
  squeezed lemon juice
1 teaspoon baking
  powder

1/4 teaspoon salt
2 tablespoons vegetable
  oil or unsalted butter,
  melted
1 egg, lightly beaten
1 tablespoon vanilla
  extract

Preheat the oven to 375° F. Lightly grease an 8-inch square baking pan or a 1½-quart casserole.

In the baking pan or casserole, combine the peaches, 2 table-spoons of the sugar, 1 tablespoon of the flour, and the lemon juice.

In a medium-size bowl, combine the remaining sugar and flour with the baking powder and salt. In a small bowl, combine the oil or butter, egg, and vanilla. Stir the oil mixture into the dry ingredients until just combined. Spoon the batter over the peaches in the baking pan.

Bake until the peach filling bubbles and the crust is golden brown, 35 to 40 minutes. Set aside to cool 15 minutes before serving. Serve warm or at room temperature.

*For easier serving, divide the peaches and batter into 6 lightly greased 10-ounce custard cups. Bake for 25 to 30 minutes.*

*When fresh peaches are unavailable, use thawed, well-drained frozen peaches.*

# Apple Crisp

6 servings

4 cups peeled and thinly sliced apples (about 3 large apples)

½ cup firmly packed light brown sugar

1 tablespoon freshly squeezed lemon juice

1 cup apple juice or cider

1 tablespoon cornstarch

½ teaspoon apple pie spice

½ cup all-purpose flour

1 cup old-fashioned rolled oats

½ teaspoon baking powder

¼ teaspoon salt

4 tablespoons (½ stick) unsalted butter, melted

2 tablespoons chopped walnuts or pecans

In a large bowl, combine the apples, ¼ cup brown sugar, and the lemon juice. Set aside.

In a small saucepan, combine the apple juice or cider, cornstarch, and apple pie spice. Bring to a boil over medium heat. Cook, stirring constantly, until thickened and translucent; pour the apple juice mixture over the apple mixture and gently combine.

In a medium-size bowl, combine the flour, rolled oats, remaining brown sugar, the baking powder, and salt. Stir in the melted butter until the mixture forms crumbs.

Preheat the oven to 350° F. Grease an 8-inch square baking pan.

Pat half of the crumb mixture into the baking pan. Spoon the apple mixture over the crumbs, smoothing the top to make a level surface. Top with the remaining crumb mixture and the nuts.

Bake until the filling is bubbly and the topping is golden brown, 30 to 35 minutes. Cool 15 minutes before cutting. Serve warm or at room temperature.

*Seasonal Fruit Crisp:* Substitute 4 cups whole berries or sliced rhubarb, peaches, nectarines, or pears for the apples, depending upon the season. You may want to substitute water, pear juice, white grape juice, or a wine cooler for the apple juice and vary the spices depending upon the fruit you are using. Try $1/4$ teaspoon nutmeg with peaches or pears and $1/8$ teaspoon cloves with berries or rhubarb.

*Especially good when served with a scoop of vanilla yogurt, frozen yogurt, or ice cream.*

*Easy for kids to make.*

# PIES AND TARTS

With our convenient recipe for Plan-Ahead Pastry, you can impress family and guests by turning out an assortment of pies and tarts in practically no time. With rounds of already-prepared pastry from the freezer, you can quickly make our Pear Tarte Tatin, Pecan Pie, Sour Cream–Apple Pie, and Frangipane Tart. Fresh raspberries and melted chocolate in a cookie crust are a seductive combination in our unique Chocolate Berry Tart.

## Plan-Ahead Pastry

❧

Three 9-inch pie crusts

4$^1$/$_2$ cups all-purpose flour
2 teaspoons salt
2 teaspoons sugar
12 tablespoons (1$^1$/$_2$ sticks) unsalted butter

$^3$/$_4$ cup vegetable shortening
$^1$/$_2$ cup cold water
1 tablespoon white vinegar

In a large bowl, combine the flour, salt, and sugar. With a pastry blender or 2 knives, cut in the butter and shortening until the mixture resembles coarse crumbs. With a fork, stir in the water and vinegar until the mixture forms a ball of dough. Add a little more water, if necessary, to make the dough manageable.

Divide the dough into 3 pieces. Shape each piece of dough into a flattened ball and roll out between pieces of wax paper to make a 12-inch round. Repeat with the remaining balls of dough. Stack the 3 dough rounds, each still in the wax paper, and wrap the stack tightly in freezer wrap. Freeze until ready to use—no longer than 6 months.

When ready to use the pastry, remove as many rounds as needed from the freezer. For the bottom crust, remove the wax paper from the frozen pastry round and place the frozen round over a 9-inch pie plate. Set aside to thaw while the filling is being prepared. For the top crust, remove only 1 piece of wax paper. When the bottom pastry has thawed, press it into the pie plate, crimp the edges, fill it, and bake according to recipe directions for the filling you are using.

If the top crust is being used, invert a second pastry round over the filling, peel off the remaining wax paper, and crimp the edges.

### Variation

*Oil-Based Pastry:* Omit the butter, shortening, and vinegar. Combine 1 cup vegetable oil and ¾ cup cold water; stir it into the flour mixture all at once to make a ball of dough. Then continue with the instructions.

*Plan-Ahead Pastry is called for in all of the following pie and tart recipes except Chocolate Berry Tart (see page 142). If you are in a hurry, you may use a round of Plan-Ahead Pastry in place of the cookie crust included in the Chocolate Berry Tart recipe.*

**PREBAKED PIE SHELL:** *Fit the thawed pastry round into the pie plate and crimp the edges. Pierce the bottom of the pastry with the tines of a fork. Line the center of the pastry shell with aluminum foil and fill with pie weights or dried beans. Preheat the oven and bake at 400°F for 15 minutes, remove the foil and weights, and bake until the center is golden, 5 to 10 minutes longer. (If beans were used for weights, they may be cooled and stored in a jar for use as weights at another time. They will not be good for eating.)*

# Chocolate Berry Tart

## Cookie Crust

- 1/4 pound (1 stick) unsalted butter, softened
- 1 tablespoon freshly grated lemon zest
- 3 tablespoons sugar
- 1 egg yolk
- 1/8 teaspoon salt
- 1 1/4 cups all-purpose flour
- 1 to 2 teaspoons ice water

## Chocolate Berry Filling

- One 3-ounce dark chocolate or milk chocolate candy bar, chopped
- 3 cups red raspberries or very small strawberries (with caps removed) or a mixture of small berries
- 2 tablespoons seedless red raspberry preserves, melted and cooled to room temperature
- 2 tablespoons fruit-flavored liqueur

Preheat the oven to 350° F.

*To make Cookie Crust:* In a medium-size bowl, with a fork, beat together the butter, lemon zest, sugar, egg yolk, and salt until well blended. Add the flour all at once and stir until a stiff dough forms. Add some ice water only if necessary to make the dough manageable.

Press the dough into a 9-inch fluted tart pan. Pierce the center of the tart shell with the tines of a fork. Bake until golden, 15 to 20 minutes. Remove from the oven.

*To make Chocolate Berry Filling:* Immediately spread ³⁄₄ of the chocolate on the bottom of the tart shell. Cool to room temperature on a wire rack.

Just before serving, melt the remaining chocolate in a microwave or in a custard cup placed in a pan of very hot water. If the chocolate in the bottom of the tart shell has hardened, warm the shell in a microwave or oven just until the chocolate softens. In a medium-size bowl, toss the berries, preserves, and liqueur. Spoon the berry mixture into the tart shell and drizzle with the melted chocolate bar. Serve immediately.

### Variations

- Use a round of Plan-Ahead Pastry (see page 140) in place of the cookie crust.
- Use ¹⁄₂-inch chunks of fresh pineapple, well drained, instead of berries.

*The secret to making this a dessert to remember is assembling it just minutes before serving it. The crust and chocolate should be slightly warm and the berries should be crisp and fresh tasting with a light coating of sweet glaze. If assembled ahead, the chocolate will harden and the sweet glaze will make the berries soft and drippy. If you prepare the chocolate-lined tart shell, the berries, and the preserves and liqueur mixture ahead but keep them separate (you can even break the last chocolate bar into a custard cup so it is ready for warming), last-minute assembly will take only minutes.*

## Pear Tarte Tatin

### 8 servings

Pear or apple tarts similar to this have been a French tradition for many years. The Tatin sisters who ran a hotel in the French countryside made the apple-version famous. The dessert later was brought to Paris, where it became a specialty at Maxime's.

To easily clean the caramelized sugar from the skillet, add several inches of water to the skillet and bring it to a boil. Allow the water to simmer until all of the caramel has melted. If some caramel is above the waterline, carefully tip the skillet until the water covers it. Discard the water, allow the skillet to cool, and wash it as usual.

**WHIPPED CREAM:** To whip cream, chill a bowl and beaters or a wire whisk. Pour the chilled cream into the bowl and whip until it becomes stiff enough to stand in peaks. If you wish, you can add 2 tablespoons confectioners' sugar and ½ teaspoon vanilla extract to the cream before beating. Because this dessert is very sweet, we suggest the unsweetened version.

³/₄ cup sugar
6 large pears, peeled and sliced
1 tablespoon unsalted butter, cut into small pieces

One 12-inch round Plan-Ahead Pastry (see page 140)
Whipped cream (optional, see page 144)

Preheat the oven to 375° F.

Heat the sugar over medium heat in a small heavy skillet, stirring occasionally, until it melts and caramelizes to a golden brown. Pour the caramelized sugar into a 10-inch pie plate; tip the plate to coat it evenly. Arrange the pear slices in concentric circles on top of the caramel in the pie plate; dot with the pieces of butter.

Place the pastry round on top of the pear slices. Turn excess pastry over onto the top of the crust.

Bake until the crust is golden brown and the pears are tender when a knife is inserted through the pastry, 45 to 50 minutes. Remove from the oven and immediately loosen the edges of the crust. Cool 10 minutes in the pie plate, then carefully drain off any syrupy liquid into a small saucepan. Invert the tart onto a heat-proof serving plate and drizzle with the reserved syrup. If the liquid seems thin, simmer it 8 to 10 minutes, until it is syrupy and then pour it over the tart. Cool the tart to room temperature and serve with whipped cream, if desired.

# Pecan Pie

### 6 servings

1 cup light corn syrup

3 eggs

½ cup granulated sugar

¼ cup firmly packed light brown sugar

2 tablespoons unsalted butter, melted

1 tablespoon all-purpose flour

2 teaspoons vanilla extract

¼ teaspoon salt

2 cups coarsely chopped pecans

Unbaked 9-inch Plan-Ahead Pastry shell (see page 140), with high, crimped rim

½ cup pecan halves

Preheat the oven to 350° F.

In a large bowl, beat together the corn syrup, eggs, granulated sugar, brown sugar, butter, flour, vanilla, and salt until well blended. Fold in the chopped pecans.

Carefully pour the pecan mixture into the pastry shell. Arrange the pecan halves over the top.

Bake until the center appears set when the pie plate is gently tapped, 45 to 50 minutes. Remove the pie to a wire rack and allow it to cool completely before cutting it.

### Variation

*Pecan Fruit Pie:* Substitute ½ cup dried currants, blueberries, cherries, or cranberries for ½ cup of the chopped pecans.

*It is a good idea to make the crimped pastry edge at least ½ inch high for Pecan Pie in order to prevent the filling from running over in the oven.*

*There are many ways to decoratively crimp the edges of a pastry shell. First, fold any excess pastry under and form a pastry rim about ¼ to ½ inch high on the rim of the pie plate. Then you can press the sides of your thumb and forefinger into the pastry ridge and pinch, or you can hold your thumb and forefinger at the outside edge of the pastry rim and press the pastry into them with the forefinger of the other hand. Perhaps the easiest is to press ridges into the pastry rim with the floured tines of a fork.*

**PEARS HÉLÈNE:** *For a simple dessert, serve poached pears topped with vanilla ice cream or frozen yogurt and Chocolate Sauce (see page 12).*

**PEAR MELBA:** *Serve poached pears topped with vanilla ice cream or frozen yogurt and Raspberry Coulis (see page 135).*

# Frangipane Tart

### 6 to 8 servings

One 12-inch Plan-Ahead Pastry (see page 140)

## Frangipane

| | |
|---|---|
| ¼ pound (1 stick) unsalted butter, softened | 1 cup (about 6 ounces) ground unblanched or toasted blanched almonds |
| ½ cup superfine sugar | ¼ cup all-purpose flour |
| 2 eggs | 1 teaspoon almond extract |

## Poached Pears

| | |
|---|---|
| 1 cup water | 3 to 4 firm pears, pared, halved, and cored |
| ½ cup granulated sugar | 1 vanilla bean, split |

## Glaze

| | |
|---|---|
| 6 tablespoons apricot preserves | 2 tablespoons water |

The Weekend Kitchen

Preheat the oven to 375° F.

Fit the pastry into the bottom and up the sides of an 8-inch tart pan with a removable bottom. Pierce the bottom with a fork.

*To make Frangipane:* Beat the butter with the sugar using a wire whisk. Beat in the eggs, one at a time, beating well after each addition, then stir in the almonds, flour, and almond extract. Turn into the pastry and bake until cooked through, about 25 minutes. Cool.

*To make Poached Pears:* While the tart is baking, bring the water and sugar to a boil, add the pears and vanilla bean, and cook until the pears are tender, 20 to 25 minutes. Remove the vanilla bean. Cool the pears in the liquid. Drain well before using.

*To make Glaze:* Heat the preserves and water.

Brush over the top of the cooled tart, attractively arrange the pear halves, then brush with the remaining glaze.

### Variation

*Chocolate Frangipane Tart:* Omit the poached pears and glaze. Melt 1 cup semisweet chocolate chips and drizzle over the cooled filling.

*If time is short, use drained, canned pears instead of the poached ones.*

*The vanilla bean can be used again. Just rinse and dry it, then—if desired—store it in your sugar canister to infuse the sugar with the essence of vanilla.*

# Sour Cream–Apple Pie

*This pie is best when served on the day it is baked.*

6 servings

½ cup sugar

½ cup all-purpose flour

¾ teaspoon ground cinnamon

¼ teaspoon salt

1 cup sour cream

1 egg

2 teaspoons vanilla extract

3 cups peeled and coarsely chopped apples (about 3 medium-size apples)

Unbaked 9-inch Plan-Ahead Pastry shell (see page 140)

¼ cup firmly packed light brown sugar

1½ tablespoons unsalted butter, melted

Preheat the oven to 350° F.

In a large bowl, stir together the sugar, 2 tablespoons of the flour, ¼ teaspoon of the cinnamon, and the salt. Add the sour cream, egg, and vanilla and beat until well blended. Fold in the apples.

Fit the pastry into a 9-inch pie plate as directed on page 141. Spoon the apple mixture into the pastry shell. In a small bowl, stir together the remaining flour, the brown sugar, the remaining cinnamon, and the melted butter, forming crumbs. Sprinkle the crumbs over the apple mixture.

Bake until the filling is set when the pie plate is gently tapped, 50 to 55 minutes. Remove the pie to a wire rack and cool completely before cutting. Refrigerate any leftovers.

### Variation

*Sour Cream–Berry or –Cherry Pie:* Substitute fresh blueberries or pitted sweet cherries for the apples.

# BREADS

Cinnamon
Coffee Cake

Bears for
Breakfast

Farmers' Market
Goat Cheese
Bread

Basic Muffins

Flaky Biscuits

Pumpernickel
Bread

Sticky Buns

Bread making is one of the most rewarding uses of relaxed weekend hours. Whether you make quick breads such as our Flaky Biscuits, Cinnamon Coffee Cake, or Basic Muffins (or one of the many biscuit and muffin variations) or you choose a yeast-raised bread such as our Farmers' Market Goat Cheese Bread, Pumpernickel Bread, or Sticky Buns, the results will delight family and friends.

 *This coffee cake is best when served the day it is baked.*

# Cinnamon Coffee Cake

9 servings

| | |
|---|---|
| 2 cups all-purpose flour | 2 teaspoons baking powder |
| ³/₄ cup firmly packed light brown sugar | 2 teaspoons ground cinnamon |
| 4 tablespoons (¹/₂ stick) unsalted butter, melted, or vegetable oil | ¹/₄ teaspoon salt |
| | 1 egg |
| | 1 cup milk |

Preheat the oven to 375° F. Lightly grease a 9-inch square baking pan.

In a medium-size bowl, stir together the flour, brown sugar, and melted butter or vegetable oil until crumbs form. Remove ¹/₂ cup and set aside.

Stir the baking powder, cinnamon, and salt into the remaining crumb mixture. Add the egg and milk and stir until just combined. Spoon the batter into the greased pan and top with the reserved crumbs.

Bake until a cake tester inserted into the center comes out clean, 25 to 30 minutes. Remove to a wire rack and let stand at least 15 minutes before cutting. Cut into squares and serve warm.

## Bears for Breakfast

Making yeast bread is a wonderful activity for children. They can learn about providing the right conditions of moisture, warmth, and sugar for the yeast so it will grow and provide the carbon dioxide that raises the dough. Kneading and shaping the dough is just as much fun as working with modeling clay, and the resulting loaf of teddy-bear bread makes a great breakfast.

Use our recipe for Farmers' Market Goat Cheese Bread (see page 152) but omit the cheese. After the first rising, give each child a batch of dough and a cookie sheet. Let the children lightly grease the center of the cookie sheet. This will also grease their hands, which will make handling the dough easier.

Divide the dough into 3 balls. Pat the first ball out to make a circle in the center of the cookie sheet for the body. Divide the second ball of dough into 4 pieces. Moisten one side of each piece and attach the pieces to the body to make teddy bear paws. Pinch a small piece of dough off of the remaining ball, then position the large piece above the body for the head. Moisten the small piece you pinched off and place it on the head for a nose. Pinch the top of the head on each side to make ears. Use raisins and dried fruit to give the bears eyes and to decorate them. Set the teddy-bear breads aside to rise, and bake according to the recipe for the Farmers' Market Goat Cheese Bread.

# Farmers' Market Goat Cheese Bread

❧

8 servings

3½ to 4 cups unbleached all-purpose flour

1 package (2 teaspoons) fast-rising dry yeast

1 teaspoon salt

1 cup hot water (120° F to 125° F)

2 tablespoons olive oil

1 tablespoon firmly packed light brown sugar

Milk

One 4-ounce package fresh goat cheese (chèvre)

1 teaspoon fresh thyme leaves or snipped fresh dill

Combine 3½ cups flour, the yeast, and salt in a large bowl. Combine the water, oil, and sugar in a glass measuring cup; stir until the sugar has dissolved. Stir the water mixture into the flour mixture until a soft smooth dough forms.

Turn the dough out onto a lightly floured board and knead for 5 minutes, adding as much of the remaining ½ cup flour as necessary to make the dough manageable. Shape the dough into a ball on the board and cover it with the bowl. Let rise until double in bulk, 20 to 25 minutes.

When the dough has risen, grease a 12- × 6-inch oval in the center of a cookie sheet. Roll out the dough to make a 10-inch square. Brush the top of the dough with a little milk. Crumble the goat cheese over the dough and sprinkle with either fresh thyme or dill. Roll up the dough jelly-roll fashion to make a 12- × 5-inch loaf. Place the loaf, open side down, on the greased baking sheet. Cut an "X" in the center of the loaf and brush the whole loaf with milk. Cover the loaf lightly with a linen towel and set aside in a warm place to rise until double in bulk, 30 to 35 minutes.

Preheat the oven to 375° F. Bake the loaf until it sounds hollow when gently tapped on the top, 35 to 40 minutes. Remove the loaf to a wire rack to cool to room temperature. Do not cut the loaf until it has cooled at least 30 minutes. To serve, cut into 8 thick slices.

*Chèvre is a mild flavored, soft, unripened cheese that is made from goat's milk. It is usually sold in "buttons" or logs and can be found rolled in herbs, pepper, or ashes. Any of the variations is delicious in this bread. If you cannot find chèvre, you could substitute 4 ounces of cream cheese or 4 ounces of a semisoft herb- and garlic-flavored cheese.*

1 dozen regular (2½-inch) or 4 giant (3½-inch) muffins

2½ cups all-purpose flour
½ cup sugar
1 tablespoon baking powder
¼ to ½ teaspoon salt
1 egg or 2 egg whites, well beaten

1 cup milk
4 tablespoons (½ stick) unsalted butter, melted, or light olive oil
1 teaspoon vanilla extract

Preheat the oven to 400° F. Grease twelve 2½-inch or four 3½-inch muffin-pan cups.

Combine the flour, sugar, baking powder, and salt to taste in a large bowl. In a separate bowl, combine the egg or egg whites, milk, melted butter or oil, and vanilla (or other extracts and flavorings when making variations). Beat together until well blended. Make a well in the dry ingredients. Pour the liquid ingredients in all at once. Stir gently until the dry ingredients are just moistened.

Fill the prepared muffin-pan cups two-thirds full. Bake until the muffins are nicely browned and a toothpick inserted in the center comes out clean, 20 to 25 minutes for regular muffins and 25 to 30 minutes for giant muffins. Remove the muffin pan to a cooling rack. Let the muffins remain in the pan a few minutes, then remove them to a linen napkin–lined basket.

*Be careful not to overbeat muffin batter; it should have a rough, lumpy appearance. Overbeating causes tough muffins with large tunnels.*

*The batter for any of these muffins can be baked in an 8-inch square pan (400°F for 20 to 25 minutes) or an 8-inch loaf pan (350°F for 40 to 45 minutes).*

*Muffins freeze well. These recipes make 12 regular muffins, so there will be leftovers. Individually wrap each muffin and place in a well-labeled freezer container or reusable plastic bag. For a quick breakfast, remove one from its wrappings, place it on a microwave-safe bread plate, and microwave on high power for about 35 seconds. For a lunchtime treat, pack a frozen muffin. It will thaw in several hours and will help to keep other things in your lunch cool.*

When making variations, stir alternate dry ingredients, spices, fruits, vegetables, and nuts into the dry ingredients before adding the liquids.

*Apple-Bran Muffins:* Substitute ½ cup oat bran or unprocessed wheat bran for ½ cup of the flour. Stir 1 cup peeled and coarsely chopped apple and ½ teaspoon ground cinnamon or apple-pie spice into the dry ingredients.

*Blueberry Muffins:* Stir 1 cup fresh or dry-pack frozen blueberries (or other berries) and ¼ teaspoon freshly grated nutmeg into the dry ingredients.

*Corn Muffins:* Substitute ¾ cup yellow cornmeal for ¾ cup of the flour. Reduce the sugar to 1 tablespoon.

*Cranberry-Orange Muffins:* Substitute ½ cup orange juice for ½ cup of the milk. Add ½ cup coarsely chopped cranberries and 1 teaspoon grated orange zest to the dry ingredients.

*Gingerbread Muffins:* Reduce the sugar to ¼ cup. Substitute ¼ cup light molasses for ¼ cup of the milk. Add 3 teaspoons ground ginger to the dry ingredients. Fold in ⅓ cup dark seedless raisins.

*Raisin Crumb Muffins:* Stir ¼ cup seedless raisins into the dry ingredients. Combine ⅓ cup flour, ¼ cup firmly packed light brown sugar, and ½ teaspoon ground cinnamon in a small bowl. Stir in 2 tablespoons melted unsalted butter or light olive oil to form crumb topping. Divide crumb topping over batter in pans.

*Texas Corn Muffins:* Add ¼ cup grated cheddar cheese or ½ cup corn kernels or 2 tablespoons well-drained chopped jalapeño pepper or all three.

# Flaky Biscuits

Ten 2-inch biscuits

2 cups all-purpose flour

1 tablespoon baking powder

1 teaspoon sugar

¼ teaspoon cream of tartar

¼ teaspoon salt

¼ cup vegetable shortening

¾ cup milk

Preheat the oven to 425° F.

In a medium-size bowl, stir together the flour, baking powder, sugar, cream of tartar, and salt. With a pastry blender or 2 knives, cut the shortening into the flour mixture until it resembles cornmeal. Stir the milk into the flour mixture until a ball of dough forms.

On a lightly floured board, roll the dough out to ¾-inch thickness. With a floured 2½-inch round cookie cutter, cut out as many dough rounds as possible; pat the scraps of dough together and cut more rounds until all the dough has been used.

Place the rounds on an ungreased baking sheet; pierce the tops with the tines of a fork several times and bake until golden brown, 12 to 14 minutes. Serve immediately.

*Pecan Biscuits:* Add ⅓ cup finely chopped pecans to the dry ingredients.

*Cheese Biscuits:* Add ½ cup coarsely shredded cheddar or Jarlsberg cheese to the dry ingredients.

*Drop Biscuits:* Increase milk to 1 cup. Drop the dough onto greased baking sheets from a tablespoon rather than rolling out and cutting the dough.

*Scones:* Add ¼ cup dried currants to the dry ingredients. Roll the dough out to make a 6-inch square. Cut the dough into quarters. Cut each quarter in half diagonally to make 8 triangles.

*Griddle Scones:* Prepare Drop Biscuits, adding ¼ cup raisins to the dough. Drop the dough by heaping tablespoonfuls onto a greased griddle. Spread the dough around to make a 2½-inch round. Bake on a griddle until golden on one side. Turn and bake until golden on the other side. Repeat to make 10 to 12 scones in all.

*For a head start on morning biscuit making, the night before combine the dry ingredients and shortening in a bowl and cover tightly. In the morning, just stir in the milk, and you are ready to bake.*

*For campfire cooking, select a biscuit or scone recipe; combine the dry ingredients and shortening in a plastic bag. When ready to bake, carefully add milk to the ingredients in the bag. Tie a knot in the top of the bag or hold it together tightly and knead until the ingredients are combined. Bake in a cast-iron griddle over the fire following the directions for Griddle Scones.*

# Pumpernickel Bread

8 to 10 servings

2 to 2½ cups bread or all-purpose flour

1¼ cups rye flour

¼ cup cornmeal

2 tablespoons unsweetened cocoa powder

1 package (2 teaspoons) fast-rising dry yeast

1 teaspoon salt

1 cup hot water (120° F to 125° F)

2 tablespoons olive oil

2 tablespoons dark molasses

Milk

½ teaspoon caraway seeds (optional)

Combine 2 cups bread flour or all-purpose flour, the rye flour, cornmeal, cocoa, yeast, and salt in a large bowl. Combine the water, oil, and molasses in a glass measuring cup; stir until the molasses and water are well blended. Stir the water mixture into the flour mixture until a soft smooth dough forms.

Turn the dough out onto a lightly floured board and knead for 5 minutes, adding as much of the remaining ½ cup bread flour or all-purpose flour as necessary to make the dough manageable. Shape the dough into a ball on the board and cover it with the bowl. Let rise until double in bulk, 30 to 35 minutes.

When the dough has risen, grease a 10-inch round in the center of a cookie sheet. Shape the dough into an 8-inch round loaf; place it on the greased baking sheet. Brush the top of the loaf with a little milk and, if desired, sprinkle it with caraway seeds. Cover the loaf lightly with a linen towel and set aside in a warm place to rise until double in bulk, 40 to 45 minutes.

Preheat the oven to 375° F.

Bake the loaf for 35 to 40 minutes or until it sounds hollow when gently tapped on the top. Remove the loaf to a wire rack to cool to room temperature. To serve, slice crosswise, then cut the larger slices in half.

## Variations

*Half-Pumpernickel Bread:* Omit the cocoa from the Pumpernickel Bread recipe and prepare the dough as directed. Before the first rising divide the dough into 2 equal pieces. Knead 1 ounce melted unsweetened chocolate and 2 to 3 tablespoons extra bread flour into one piece of the dough. Raise the doughs separately. To shape the loaf, roll out each dough to form an 8-inch square. Brush the tops of the squares with water. Place 1 dough square on top of the other and roll them up jelly-roll fashion to make a 10- × 5-inch loaf. Allow to rise and bake as directed for Pumpernickel Bread.

*Pumpernickel Raisin:* Prepare the dough as directed for Pumpernickel Bread, stirring in ⅓ cup dark seedless raisins with the water mixture. Shape and bake as for Pumpernickel Bread or form into 10 to 12 round rolls and reduce rising and baking times by 15 to 20 minutes.

*Fast-rising dry yeast is an entirely different variety of yeast from the traditional one found in compressed yeast or the regular active dry yeast. It produces carbon dioxide more quickly than the other yeast and raises dough in about half the time. It is easier to use because the yeast works well when mixed with dry ingredients (this eliminates the yeast-softening step), and it can tolerate very warm water (you are less likely to kill the yeast).*

*To use regular active dry yeast in any of these recipes, soften the yeast for several minutes in the liquid called for in the recipe (no hotter than 105°F to 115°F) and add it to the dry ingredients. Double the rising times called for in the recipe.*

*Both fast-rising and active dry yeast may be purchased in either ¼-ounce (7-gram) packages or in bulk jars. Each package contains about 2 teaspoons of yeast and can take the place of 1 compressed yeast cake (sometimes called for in older recipes).*

# Sticky Buns

〜⊙

9 servings

3½ to 4 cups unbleached all-purpose flour

3 tablespoons granulated sugar

1 package (2 teaspoons) fast-rising dry yeast

1 teaspoon salt

1¼ cups milk, scalded and cooled to 125° F

4 tablespoons (½ stick) butter, melted

½ cup dark seedless raisins

½ cup coarsely chopped walnuts or pecans

¼ cup firmly packed light brown sugar

½ teaspoon ground cinnamon

¾ cup maple syrup or pancake syrup

Combine 3½ cups flour, the granulated sugar, yeast, and salt in a large bowl. Add the milk and 3 tablespoons of the melted butter to the flour mixture; stir until a soft, smooth dough forms.

Turn the dough out onto a lightly floured board and knead for 5 minutes, adding as much of the remaining ½ cup flour as necessary to make the dough manageable. Shape the dough into a ball on the board and cover it with the bowl. Let rise until double in bulk, 20 to 25 minutes.

When the dough has risen, grease a 9-inch square baking pan. Roll out the dough to make a 12-inch square. Brush the top of the dough with the remaining melted butter. For the topping, sprinkle ¼ cup raisins, ¼ cup chopped nuts, 2 tablespoons light brown sugar, and the cinnamon over the dough. Roll up the dough, jelly-roll fashion; cut crosswise into 9 equal pieces. Sprinkle the remaining raisins, nuts, and light brown sugar over the bottom of the greased pan. Drizzle the syrup over the top. Place the buns in the pan with the cut sides up. Lightly cover the pan and set aside in a warm place to rise until double in bulk, 30 to 35 minutes.

Preheat the oven to 350° F.

Bake the Sticky Buns for 35 to 40 minutes or until they sound hollow when gently tapped on the top. Remove the pan from the oven; loosen the edges of the buns with a kitchen knife and immediately invert onto a heat-proof serving plate, being careful not to let the hot syrup touch your hands. Cool for 20 to 30 minutes before serving. To serve, cut or pull apart into 9 buns.

### Variation

For individual servings, divide the topping into nine 2½- or 3-inch muffin-pan cups and place 1 piece of rolled dough into each. Set the pan on a cookie sheet, let rise, and bake as directed for 20 to 25 minutes.

# INDEX